BEGINNER'S GUIDE TO HOME COMPUTERS

BEGINNER'S GUIDE TO
HOME COMPUTERS

Marvin Grosswirth

Dolphin Books
DOUBLEDAY & COMPANY, INC., Garden City, New York

LIBRARY OF CONGRESS CATALOGING IN PUBLICATION DATA
GROSSWIRTH, MARVIN, 1930–
BEGINNER'S GUIDE TO HOME COMPUTERS.
BIBLIOGRAPHY: P. 105
1. MICROCOMPUTERS.   I. TITLE.   II. TITLE: HOME COMPUTERS.
QA76.5.G765   001.6'4'04
ISBN: 0-385-13572-6
LIBRARY OF CONGRESS CATALOG CARD NUMBER: 77–16918

Dedicated to

PHIL DORN

who dragged me, kicking and screaming, into the world of computers.

ACKNOWLEDGMENTS

Many people helped in the completion of this book, especially:

Philip H. Dorn, President, Dorn Computer Consultants, Inc., who has been a friend, a guide, and a mentor throughout the project; Harold L. Menzel, System Technical Specialist, Systems and Data Processing, J. C. Penney Co., Inc., an avowed microcomputer enthusiast (and worthy poker adversary) who offered a multitude of insights from the standpoint of a home computer owner and then meticulously ironed out technical wrinkles in the manuscript; Marilyn S. Grosswirth, Research Consultant, Corporate Computer Services, Equitable Life Assurance Society of the U.S., who checked and criticized the manuscript for clarity and accuracy and who developed the flowchart on page 53; Kathryn Marsala, Technical Information Specialist and Manager of the Technical Information Center at Equitable Life, who made available the resources of the Center and her own considerable research expertise; and representatives of IBM, RCA Solid State, Commodore Business Machines, Inc., Pertec Computer Corp., Simon/Public Relations, Inc., The Radio Shack, and especially Texas Instruments—all of whom responded to my pleas for help with alacrity, good humor, and a wealth of valuable material.

All of these good people have my deep gratitude for contributing significantly to this book. I am, however, solely responsible for any errors of fact or judgment that may have crept in.

New York
February 1978

M.G.

CONTENTS

CONTENTS

INTRODUCTION

It may be safely assumed that you have acquired this book because you are considering, either seriously or frivolously, the acquisition of a home computer. To someone who has no knowledge of computers and is perhaps even somewhat intimidated by them, the prospect of sharing the sanctity of one's home with such a device may appear a little frightening. Relax. In all likelihood, all you probably really need to feel comfortable about the idea of living with a computer is this book. And all you really need to be comfortable with this book is a high school education or its equivalent, and average intelligence. If you are an electronics engineer or would like to become one, take this book back to the store and see if you can get your money back: we are starting from scratch and you have already passed us by.

Similarly, if you have a particular love for numbers in general and mathematics in particular, you are likely to find this book somewhat unsatisfying. On the other hand, if you have a slight aversion to mathematics, then this book may well prove to be both a comfort and a help: discussions about mathematics have been kept to the barest possible minimum.

One of the unfortunate truisms about computers, regardless of their size, location, or use, is that a considerable and formidable jargon, almost constituting a different language, has grown up about them. Indeed, the computer field has been guilty of some of the worst atrocities ever perpetrated on the English language. Words like "retrofit" and expressions like "artificial intelligence" were coined by computer people. On the other hand, the computer field has been known to produce some worthwhile additions to the language: surely "interface" is one of the most useful and expressive verbs to be added to English in recent years. There is no escaping the jargon, and much of it, therefore, is included in this book. There is, at the back of the book, a glossary which can be resorted to in moments of stress; however, it will probably not be necessary to refer to it during the actual reading of these pages. When a new term appears, it is in *italics* and immediately defined. If there is a considerable lapse between a word's initial appearance and a recurring usage, that word again appears in italics. Everything is explained in the text and there are no footnotes to distract or bedevil you. (A once-over perusal of the Glossary is recommended as an easy and painless means of becoming acclimated to the language of the computer world.)

Beginner's Guide to Home Computers is exactly that—a guide. Its main purpose is to help you decide whether a home computer is for you. Its second purpose is to demonstrate that you need not become involved in complex and complicated electronics and mathematics to own and enjoy a personal computer. On the other hand, if you do want to plunge into the world of miniaturized circuits and sophisticated mathematical exercises, a personal computer offers the best opportunities for you . . . because chances are that they won't let you play around with the machines at the office.

BEGINNER'S GUIDE TO HOME COMPUTERS

1

WHAT IS A COMPUTER?

A computer, unless it is broken, never makes a mistake. It is simply incapable of doing so. When a clerk at the local power company or at your favorite department store or in your company's payroll department says, "The computer made a mistake," you have reason to assume that either that person is stupid or thinks you are. *The computer made a mistake* really means that a person or persons operating the computer made a mistake, either by giving the machine incorrect information or by failing to provide it with a proper set of instructions.

Similarly, when some seemingly simple and logical action on your part is thwarted by the statement, "The computer won't let us do that," do not blame the machine. Blame instead the insensitive and intransigent nincompoops who, once having programmed the computer to perform certain functions, are unable or unwilling to get their machine to do something else.

A computer is a machine. It performs arithmetic functions. Having performed these functions, it makes comparisons. Built into this machine is the capacity to remember what it has done. The machine also performs logic functions, and it can be given a set of instructions which tell it what it must do and how it

must do it. It can then produce the results that are achieved upon the completion of those instructions. It performs all of these things at an incredibly high speed.

From a purely functional point of view, it is the high speed that differentiates the computer from the human brain. Setting aside for a moment the humanistic or humanizing aspects of the brain, it can be seen that there is a considerable similarity between the machine and the human. A person is also capable of doing arithmetic, of making comparisons and remembering what he or she has done. And a person can be told what has to be done, how it is to be done and, after following the instructions, produce a desired result.

Consider, for example, a fairly commonplace cost-allocation problem, likely to arise in virtually any business situation. Suppose I have 4 people working for 17 hours at a rate of $4.82 per hour. Suppose further that there is a payroll tax of 11.4 per cent. Assume further that the total cost is to be equally divided among three separate projects. What is my total cost? What is my cost per project? With several sharp pencils, a large quantity of paper, and more endurance than I have been known to demonstrate, I would perform the following tasks:

(1) Multiply $4 \times 17 \times 4.82$.
(2) Multiply that answer by .114 (11.4%)
(3) Add the result of step (1) to the result of step (2).
(4) Divide that answer by 3.

If the telephone does not ring, if I have had a good night's sleep, and if I come up with the right answers the first time through, I would estimate that solving that problem would take me eight to twelve minutes. However, I have a hand-held calculator (which, as we shall see later, is a kind of a computer), that is a fairly simple one: it has the four basic arithmetic functions of addition, subtraction, multiplication, and division. It also has a "per cent" key that makes possible the simple and automatic calculation of percentages. All I need to do, therefore, is press the following keys on my calculator:

$$4 \times 17 \times 4.82 + 11.4\% \div 3 =$$

That operation takes about fifteen seconds. (The answer, if you care, is $365.12 for the total cost; $121.71 for each project.) Fifteen seconds vs. eight minutes represents a considerable saving in time; yet, when it comes to computers, hand-held calculators are considered agonizingly slow.

Calculating machines that enable people to rapidly perform computations are by no means a new concept. At some unknown point in antiquity, one or several of our sophisticated ancestors realized that by using some object to represent digits it might be possible to perform computations beyond the limited scope of one's own ten fingers and ten toes. Shells, chicken bones, peach pits, or any number of objects could have been used, but the fact that the word "calculate" is derived from *calculus*, the Latin word for small stone, suggests that pebbles were in great demand. Ultimately, such pebbles or beads were arranged to form the familiar abacus, the first man-made computing device. The abacus was in use for centuries, its decline coinciding more

or less with that of the Roman Empire. It was reintroduced in Europe around the year A.D. 1000, but it never regained its earlier popularity. In the Far East, however, its use has continued to this very day.

The abacus is based upon a series of vertical lines on which are strung a number of beads. The first line (counting from the right) represents units. The second line represents tens; the third, hundreds; the fourth, thousands, etc. Running horizontally through the abacus' frame is a bar. The beads above this crossbar represent fives; those below the crossbar represent ones. A Chinese abacus has two beads over the crossbar and five below the crossbar on each line. The *soroban*, the Japanese abacus, is similar in operation but has four beads below the bar and one above. By manipulating the beads, it is possible, with some skill and practice, to make rapid calculations.

In 1642, a French mathematician named Blaise Pascal invented an adding machine based on the principle of the abacus but eliminating the need to move the counters by hand. Pascal's device consisted of several wheels. Each wheel was engraved with the digits 0 through 9 and equipped with a little tab located near the 9 on the wheel's edge. When the unit's wheel was turned to 0, the little tab engaged the second wheel, turning it to number 1, so that together, the wheels displayed the number 10. When the next—the tens—wheel reached 0, its tab turned the third wheel a notch, displaying 100. And so on. Although Pascal's adding machine was invented over three centuries ago, its principle is still in use in such devices as your car's odometer or the counter on a tape recorder.

Thirty-two years later, a German with the formidable name of Gottfried Wilhelm von Leibnitz made several improvements on Pascal's machine. Thanks to Leibnitz, the device could now multiply and divide as easily as it could add and subtract. In 1850, D. D. Parmalee, an American inventor, devised a system by which properly marked keys turned the wheels, eliminating the need to do so by hand. The addition, years later, of an electric motor to Parmalee's improvement is the grandfather of the familiar adding machine.

In the meantime, there were men of vision looking far beyond the mere functions of addition, subtraction, multiplication, and division. One such forward thinker was the nineteenth-century English mathematician Charles Babbage. In the late eighteenth century, Joseph Marie Jacquard, a Frenchman, invented the mechanical loom. Jacquard's loom wove fabrics in a variety of patterns based upon "instructions" entered on a series of punched cards. In 1833, Babbage applied the punched-card concept to a machine he called his "analytical engine." Babbage envisioned a machine capable of performing virtually any mathematical operation. It would have a "memory" that could store numbers. It could make comparisons between the results of the various operations. In short, what Babbage had envisioned was the modern computer. He spent nearly four decades developing his ideas, and ultimately failed because it was impossible to produce the parts required for his machine precisely enough. Although the analytical engine was never built, it incorporated many of the elements of modern computers. What Babbage lacked was electronics.

In 1890, Herman Hollerith, working for the U. S. Census Bureau, devised a series of holes punched into cards representing the digits 0 through 9 and the letters of the alphabet. The principle of the punched card is a simple one. When the card is passed over a series of electrical contacts, the hole permits the completion of an electrical circuit. The arrangement of those electrical circuits that have been completed represents a set of instructions. The code developed by Hollerith (called, not surprisingly, the Hollerith code) is still being used.

With the Hollerith method, computerization was well on the way. In 1890, the Census Bureau used punched cards to classify the American population, cutting by two thirds the time it had taken to do the same thing ten years earlier. The success of the Census Bureau inspired other government uses for the punched-card method; and in 1911, International Business Machines (IBM) was born out of the union between a company that manufactured Hollerith's equipment and a competitive firm.

As the use of electricity became more sophisticated and technology improved, calculating machines also improved. The Burroughs adding machine made its first appearance in 1885, and in 1917, just in time for World War I, a calculator that could add, subtract, multiply, and divide came on the scene. In 1925, Vannevar Bush, an American electrical engineer, together with his colleagues, built a machine that could solve differential equations. In 1937, Howard Aiken of Harvard University, using Babbage's principles, envisioned a completely automatic electromechanical computer.

Through the combined efforts of the Harvard geniuses and IBM, the Automatic Sequence Controlled Calculator was brought to life in 1944. Christened the MARK I, it could perform addition, multiplication, subtraction, and division in any specified sequence. The MARK I could store and regurgitate tables of results it had previously computed. Information was fed into the MARK I by punched cards and by the proper setting of certain switches; MARK I typed its answers out on a typewriter or punched them onto cards. It took the system about three seconds to creak out a typical multiplication. The machine weighed about five tons; its memory contained over three thousand electromechanical relays. MARK I survived for fifteen years and was finally retired from service in 1959. Portions of its innards may be viewed at the Smithsonian Institution in Washington.

Roughly coinciding with Professor Aiken's development of the MARK I, John P. Eckert and John W. Mauchly, at the University of

Pennsylvania, struck upon the concept of using electronics as a means of obtaining the high speeds necessary to process the enormous quantities of data on ballistics and meteorological studies that were their responsibility. They designed the Electronic Numerical Integrator and Computer, which was promptly labeled by its initials, ENIAC. Their machine contained some eighteen thousand vacuum tubes, one of which was expected to fail approximately every seven-and-a-half minutes. Before very long, however, specially designed vacuum tubes enabled ENIAC to run for several days in succession without having to have one or more of its tubes replaced. ENIAC was fast: it could multiply in 2.8 milliseconds and add in 0.2 milliseconds. (A millisecond is a thousandth of a second.) For all its speed, however, it was monstrous by today's standards. In *Asimov's Guide to Science,* author Isaac Asimov writes: "Whereas ENIAC weighed thirty tons and took up 1,500 square feet of floor space, the equivalent computer today—using switching units far smaller, faster, and more reliable than the old vacuum tubes—could be built into an object the size of a refrigerator." But that was written in 1972. A mere five years later, it was possible and practical to manufacture a computer with ENIAC's capability contained in a unit that fits comfortably on a tabletop.

ENIAC was the progenitor of the modern computer. The history of development from ENIAC to computers for home use is essentially a chronology of electronic innovation, refinement, and improved production methods, as we shall see in Chapter 4.

As a matter of information, you should know that there are two types of computers: analog and digital. An *analog* computer is one which takes certain physical properties, qualities, or quantities (such as air pressure, temperature, etc.) and transforms them into varying electrical impulses. Usually, the results of the analog computer's computations are displayed graphically.

A *digital* computer, on the other hand, works wholly with numbers, and every operation, despite its being performed at inconceivably high speeds, is sequential. It is perhaps an oversimplification, but the difference between analog and digital computers can best be explained by wristwatches. You can tell the time by noting the position of the hands on a watch. It is not necessary to look at the numbers, and, indeed, some of the most popular watches have few or no numbers or markers on them other than the two hands and some indication of where twelve o'clock is. The position of the hands is an analog. A digital watch, however, is precisely that: it gives the time by displaying a series of digits.

Analog computers have been used in chemical plants to simulate flow, they have been used to demonstrate the behavior of springs under pressure, to simulate wing loadings on aircraft, and for similar approximations of various processes. Note, however, that this is written in the past tense. Analog computers are becoming scarcer and scarcer and, in the opinion of some experts, represent a vanishing species.

(This book is confined only to digital computers; therefore, now that you know the difference between an analog computer and a digital computer, you may comfortably forget about it.)

With dismaying frequency, computers are compared to the human brain. The comparison is justified only to an extent. At this very moment, you are receiving information by reading this book. That information enters your brain and may proceed along any one of several paths. It may be placed in your memory for early retrieval. For example, if you are planning to buy a computer tomorrow, then you will want to recall what you have learned today about home computers. If, however, you do not plan to purchase a computer for some time, then the information you are now receiving may be placed in another "compartment" of your memory, which, for want of a better word, we can call "storage." At some later date, you may want to retrieve that information from storage. At the same time, your brain contains other data relevant to your purchase of a computer. You know whether you have the financial resources to buy one. You know whether you have the space to accommodate one. You know (or will know by the time you finish this book) how much technical dexterity will be required to operate one and how much you are capable of delivering. When you have all the information necessary for making a decision, you will compare pieces of data and arrive at an intelligent conclusion. For example, you will compare the size of a computer with the space you have available for it and, on the basis of that comparison, determine whether you have room for the machine. You will compare the cost of the machine with the amount of money you have available and determine whether you can afford to buy it. You will have performed, in other words, what in the computer world is referred to as *data processing*. Data processing means taking a quantity of information—*data* —and performing a systematic and sequential series of operations, either mathematically or logically or both. In other words, processing the data.

A computer also processes data. It can take information and, by performing mathematical and/or logical operations, arrive at a conclusion and make a decision. For example, if you feed into the computer the price of the device you are interested in buying and your total financial resources, and then feed in your total expenses, the computer will be able to add all of your expenses, deduct that total from your available financial resources, compare the remainder with the price of the computer you want to buy and then make a decision. If there is enough left over, the computer will tell you to go out and buy. If there is not enough left over, the computer will tell you not to buy. So far, so good: as we discussed earlier, the computer can do what the human brain can do, except much faster.

Thus, the computer may be said to be equivalent to a human brain. However, the computer has no mind. More than one commentator has described a computer as an idiot. It can do only what it is told to do and only how it is told to do it. If you are trying to decide, for example, between the purchase of an encyclopedia and a home computer, no calculating machine, however sophisticated, can tell you which is better for furthering the education of your children or honing their intellects. One of the sadder absurdities that has evolved with the evolution of computer technology is computer crime. It has often been stated that the computer is the perfect partner in crime because it has no morals, it can keep a secret, it does exactly what it is told, and it has no loyalty. In every instance where crime-by-computer has been brought to light, the exposure was the result of human rather than machine failure.

Despite science fiction to the contrary, the likelihood of computers taking over the world is slim at best. The computer is a tool of humankind. It is an efficient tool and one which has certainly changed everyone's life.

As the cliché so aptly puts it, the computer's usefulness for good or evil depends not on the machine but on who is manipulating it.

2

HOW COMPUTERS WORK

• The Basic Elements

Let's carry our analogy between a computer and a human being just a bit further. The complex machine we call a computer consists of only four basic elements: (1) the central processing unit, (2) storage, (3) input, and (4) output.

The *central processing unit,* or, as it is more familiarly known, the *CPU,* is the computer's "brain." Its name is actually quite descriptive of its function. It is inside the CPU that instructions are decoded and the arithmetic is done. The CPU also controls the functioning of the other parts of the computer.

Storage is the computer's *memory.* The computer can "store" the instructions which it has been given in its memory. It can also "remember" the data which has been given to the computer as well as the answers to previously solved problems.

As in the human brain, the computer's memory, or storage, can be separated into two general categories: main and auxiliary. The *main storage* retains instructions and information necessary for the specific task being performed at the moment. *Auxiliary storage* holds information that is likely to be used, and is therefore more or less permanently stored.

A computer can retrieve the information filed in the auxiliary storage and bring it into main storage as the need arises. (Some people call the main storage "memory" and the auxiliary storage "storage." If you find that a handy method of differentiating between the two, then by all means use it. Essentially, however, "memory" and "storage" are synonymous.)

Input and *output* are, in effect, the eyes, ears, and mouth of the computers. An *input device* is one which enables you to put instructions and information—or data—into the computer. Typically, an input device consists of a typewriter-like keyboard, a keypad similar to that of a hand-held calculator or a push-button telephone, a tape reader, or various other kinds of devices.

An *output device* is one which the computer uses to relay its findings—a video screen, a typewriter, a printer, or some other device. Obviously, some of these objects can be used for both input and output. Frequently, therefore, input and output devices are categorized together and indicated by the symbol *I/O*. One of the more offensive linguistic abominations perpetrated by the computer industry is the use of "input" and "output" as verbs. Thus, one inputs data to the computer, which then outputs the result. (I/O devices, also known as *peripherals,* are discussed at greater length in the next chapter.)

● The Binary System

If the CPU is the brain of the computer, then electricity is its blood. Electricity always travels in a complete circuit. It emanates from a source, travels through some "resistance," and returns to the source. "Resistance" can be visualized as an impediment in the circuit that draws off some of the electricity for the performance of some function. For example, if you are reading this book by artificial light, the lamp is a resistance through which the electricity must flow. When you turn off the lamp by flipping a switch, you break the circuit. A computer contains thousands of tiny circuits, each of which is used to perform a specific function. Some circuits are used for addition, some for subtraction; others hold instructions or retain numbers. The function and location of each circuit are "known" by the CPU.

The fact that electricity flows in a circuit is basic to the operation of a computer and to the conveyance of information. Let us have another look at your reading lamp. Your lamp is either on or off. If it is on, the bulb is glowing and you can tell that the lamp is on. If it is off, the bulb is dark and you know that the lamp is off. That is, of course, simple almost to the point of idiocy. But as you will soon see, that actually provides a considerable amount of data. If the bulb were not in the lamp, you could still tell whether it was on or off by the position of the switch. If the switch were inaccessible, and there was no bulb in the lamp, you could *still* determine whether the lamp was on or off by inserting your finger in the socket (although whether the information is worth the price is something else again).

Now, let us assume that you have not one, but four reading lamps neatly arranged in a straight line. In your imagination, label the lamp at the extreme right with the number 1. Label the next lamp number 2, the next number 4, and the one at the extreme left number 8. Turn off all the lamps. You should now have an arrangement approximately resembling this sketch:

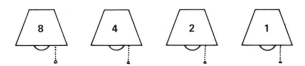

Now, you can represent any of the four digits shown merely by turning on the appropriate lamp. You can also represent several other values by turning on combinations of lamps. For example, you could represent the value of 3 by turning on lamps 1 and 2, the value of 10 by turning on lamps 8 and 2, the value of 12 by turning on lamps 8 and 4, the value of 15 by turning on all the lamps, etc. What we have here, then, are definitions of two essential aspects to the function of a computer. First, we have a working definition of *electronics.* This often-used and much-abused word simply means the transmittal of information by means of electricity. The on-off states of the lamps also give us the basis for a numbering system known as *binary numbering.* Before delving into the binary system, it may be useful to briefly review our more common method of numbering, the decimal system.

The *decimal system* is a base-10 system. That means that it is based on the number 10. Consider, for example, the number 4,376. We know, from its place in that series, that the 6 represents units; in other words, it is in the 1's column. Immediately to the left is the 10's column, so the 7 is really 7 times 10, or 70. The 3 is in the 100's column and represents 300, and the 4 is in the 1,000's column and represents 4,000. Should it be necessary to do so, we could, theoretically, continue adding digits to the left of the 4, and each successive place would represent a value ten times greater than the one immediately preceding it. With that in mind, let us return to the binary system.

Binary means base-2; 2 is the only number base that a device which depends on the flow of electricity can use, because electricity is either on or off; therefore, those are the only two states to which values can be assigned. To be specific, if we go back to our lamps, we can say that when a lamp is on it has a value of 1. When it is off it has a value of 0. In the decimal system, each place has a value ten times greater than the place immediately preceding it. In the binary system, each place has a value double the one preceding it. Presumably, therefore, we could continue to add to our string of lamps. A lamp to the left of the one numbered 8 would have a value of 16, a lamp to the left of that would have a value of 32, the next one would have a value of 64, and so on.

Now let's transfer this concept to the innards of a computer. Obviously, a computer packed full of reading lamps is impractical. There is instead an arrangement of electrical impulses which are turned on or off depending upon the number to be represented. If "off" means 0 and "on" means 1, then a number can be represented by arranging ones and zeros accordingly. For example, the binary character 0110 can be used to represent the value of 6. The 0 on the extreme right, being "off," has no value. The 1 in the place second from the right has a value of 2. The 1 to the left of that has a value of 4, and the 0 at the extreme left has no value. The 4 and the 2 equal 6. That configuration, 0110, always means 6 to the computer. The computer can store it, can use it to perform arithmetic functions, shift it around as necessary, and display it as a 6. These representations (on=1, off=0) are called *bits* (contraction for *b*inary digi*t*). The grouping of bits, such as 0110 to represent number 6, is called a *character*.

The number of bits in a character never changes. In any given computer, all the characters have the same number of bits. Establishing the number of bits in a character produces a *code*—i.e. a set of characters each of which has a fixed number of bits. This code is, in effect, the computer's own language, the medium through which the computer talks to itself. In a sense, the code can be compared to an alphabet. In our alphabet, we use this symbol—B—to represent a certain sound. To effectively communicate in our language, that symbol must always represent that sound. In some other alphabet, this same sound may be represented by a completely different symbol, but it must be consistent in its representation within that alphabet and any language that uses that alphabet. So an alphabet is, after all, just another form of code.

By combining the principle of "on" representing 1 and "off" representing 0 with the binary number system, we see that a four-bit character can represent 0 through 15, or 0000 through 1111. But in our decimal system, only ten single-place digits—0 through 9—are required. To enable a computer to use the binary system to represent the decimal system, a set of characters—a code—was derived from the binary system and used to convey the digital values of the decimal system. It is called, not surprisingly, *Binary Coded Decimal,* or *BCD*. BCD uses four bits representing 1, 2, 4, and 8 (remember the lamps?), and two "zone bits" which allow the coding of addition characters.

But BCD only provides sixty-four characters—the digits 0 through 9, the alphabet, punctuation, and some special-purpose characters. As a code, the BCD is adequate, but somewhat limiting in its size.

As a result, a method was found to extend the codes. One such extended code is the *Extended Binary Coded Decimal Interchange Code.* (Surely it will not surprise you by now to learn that this is abbreviated as EBCDIC, and pronounced EBB-SEE-DIK.) The EBC-

DIC code uses two four-bit characters in tandem for each representation. The first four bits comprise a *classification character*. The other four bits are used for the character itself. There are sixteen classifications, each of which contains sixteen characters, for a total of 256 characters. When the computer "reads" the classification character, it can tell what the next four bits will represent. Thus, a four-bit character may represent a digit or a letter or a mathematical function. Its specific application is determined by the classification character which precedes it.

This method of extended coding provides for 52 alphabetical characters (the alphabet in upper and lower case), the digits 0 through 9, punctuation and other signs and symbols, and various controls and directions within the central processing unit. In all, some 150 characters are coded in EBCDIC, leaving the remaining 106 characters available for a wide variety of special functions.

Strictly speaking, the bit patterns in the EBCDIC are not exactly characters because they consist of two elements—the classification function and the information function. This type of character is known as a *byte*. (I have no idea why.)

Sometimes, a computer moves around a unit consisting of half a byte, or four bits. In what can only be seen as an excess of cuteness, these half-bytes are referred to as *nibbles* (except by those who can never leave bad enough alone and prefer *nybbles*).

The EBCDIC code was developed by IBM for its System/360 computer, a system in extensive use in commerce and industry. It is, therefore, one of the most popular, but by no means the only, code in existence.

Codes are concerned chiefly with the inner workings of the machinery, so the chances of your becoming directly involved with them are somewhat remote. If you become intimate with your computer and want to make some changes or adjustments in the code, the manu-

Number Systems Equivalents

Decimal	Hexadecimal	Octal	Binary
0	0	0	0000
1	1	1	0001
2	2	2	0010
3	3	3	0011
4	4	4	0100
5	5	5	0101
6	6	6	0110
7	7	7	0111
8	8	10	1000
9	9	11	1001
10	A	12	1010
11	B	13	1011
12	C	14	1100
13	D	15	1101
14	E	16	1110
15	F	17	1111

facturer of the equipment can undoubtedly supply you with the information you will need.

There are two more numbering systems you ought to know about, although at first you will probably not be using them. Clearly, the binary numbering system leaves considerable room for error, particularly in long numbers where the 1's and 0's can easily become transposed and where such transposition is likely to go undetected. To minimize such errors and to increase the speed with which programs can be written, the octal and hexadecimal numbering systems are used. The *octal* is a base-8 system; the *hexadecimal* is a base-16 system. A table summarizing the equivalents in hexadecimal, decimal, octal, and binary number systems is shown above. As you can see, the hexadecimal system employs the letters A through F in addition to digits. Octal and hexadecimal numbers are indicated by subscripts. Thus, a number like $57,201_8$ is an octal number; $87ADF4_{16}$ is a hexadecimal number.

The octal and hexadecimal systems are used as a kind of shorthand for writing binary numbers.

ASCII Code Conversion Chart

SECOND HEXADECIMAL DIGIT

	0	1	2	3	4	5	6	7	8	9	A	B	C	D	E	F
0	*NUL	SOH	STX	ETX	EOT	ENQ	ACK	BEL	BS	HT	LF	VT	FF	CR	CO	SI*
1	*DLE	DC1	DC2	DC3	DC4	NAK	SYN	ETB	CAN	EM	SUB	ESC	FS	GS	ES	US*
2	SP	!	"	#	$	%	&	'	(	)	*	+	,	-	.	/
3	0	1	2	3	4	5	6	7	8	9	:	;	<	=	>	?
4	@	A	B	C	D	E	F	G	H	I	J	K	L	M	N	O
5	P	Q	R	S	T	U	V	W	X	Y	Z	[	\	]	|	—
6	\	a	b	c	d	e	f	g	h	i	j	k	l	m	n	o
7	p	q	r	s	t	u	v	w	x	y	z	⟨	|	⟩	~	DEL

(FIRST HEXADECIMAL DIGIT — rows labeled 0 through 7 at left)

Several books prepared for computer hobbyists and enthusiasts discuss octal and hexadecimal numbering systems in some detail (see Bibliography). The likelihood of your having to trouble yourself with such mathematical niceties, however, is slim, at least in the early stages of your involvement with your own home computer.

A particularly important code is the *ASCII* (for American Standard Code for Information Interchange). This code is used by computers to permit the interchange between the I/O devices and the central processing unit. ASCII can be written in several ways. The chart above shows the ASCII written in the hexadecimal numbering system, but it can be converted to the octal numbering system.

Thus, to translate the letter W into ASCII code, look on the chart for the letter W. You will find that it is in horizontal Row 5. Vertically on the chart it is equal to the number 7 under Second Hexadecimal Digit, so that the letter W written in ASCII code is 57. Reversing the process, if we see the ASCII code 3D, by checking the above chart, we find that that represents an equal sign (=).

The full ASCII code comprises 128 units, including alphanumerics, punctuation, and special symbols. *Alphanumerics,* as the construction of the word suggests, is computerese for letters and numbers. In the case of the ASCII code, the alphanumerics are all of the letters of the alphabet in both upper and lower case, and the digits 0 through 9.

● **The Central Processing Unit (CPU)**

The central processing unit has two main components. One is the *control unit,* and the other is the *arithmetic/logic unit.*

The *control unit* can reasonably be compared with the human brain. If you strike your thumb with a hammer, a signal is transmitted from the injured area to the brain, and in rapid, split-second succession, you drop the hammer, jerk your thumb away, and emit a sound which could be anything from *Ouch!* to some unprintable expletive. All of that is essentially automatic and requires no effort on your part; the brain is "programmed" to have your body react in such a manner. Now, as you gaze at your throbbing thumb, you decided that the pain and swelling might be eased by cold running water. You go into the kitchen, turn on the tap, and plunge your thumb into the soothing stream. Each one of

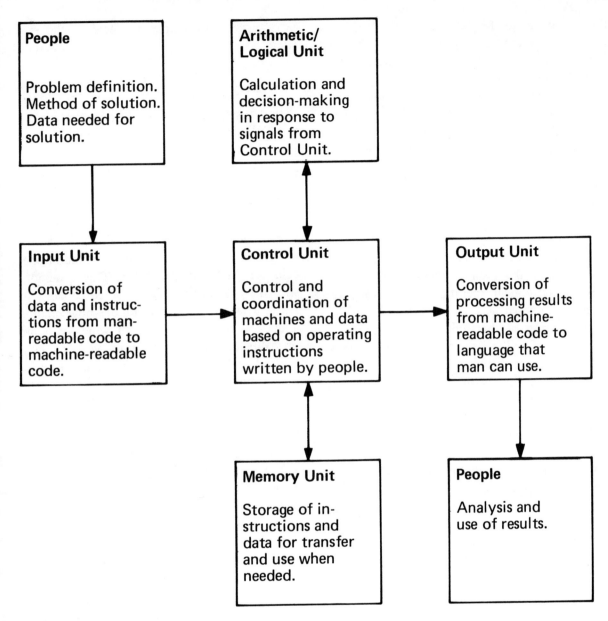

People

Problem definition.
Method of solution.
Data needed for
solution.

**Arithmetic/
Logical Unit**

Calculation and
decision-making
in response to
signals from
Control Unit.

Input Unit

Conversion of
data and instruc-
tions from man-
readable code to
machine-readable
code.

Control Unit

Control and
coordination of
machines and data
based on operating
instructions
written by people.

Output Unit

Conversion of
processing results
from machine-
readable code to
language that
man can use.

Memory Unit

Storage of in-
structions and
data for transfer
and use when
needed.

People

Analysis and
use of results.

A block diagram of a computer system. The basics
shown here are the same for any system, regardless
of size or capacity. Courtesy IBM.

those steps, from the decision to the final action, is controlled within your brain.

In approximately the same way, the control unit of the CPU controls the actions, both automatic and nonautomatic, of the computer.

The control unit in the computer receives and "understands" the orders and instructions it receives. It then converts those orders and instructions into action, turning various devices on and off, moving information around within the system, and controlling and directing the arithmetic/logic unit.

The *arithmetic/logic* (ALU) unit contains all of the circuits of a central processing unit in which, as the name suggests, the mathematical and logical operations are performed. These are known as *logic circuits.* The arithmetic portion of this unit controls addition, subtraction, multiplication, division, square root calculations, the solving of exponential problems, dealing with trigonometric functions, etc.

The logic unit consists primarily of the *accumulator.* Essentially, the accumulator is a kind of holding area. It is a temporary memory for information coming into the logic unit from the main storage. It also retains answers that are produced by the adders (which we will get to in a moment). Partial answers that must be retained while working out computations are also temporarily stored in the accumulator.

Also located among the logic circuits are the *adders.* The adder's role is almost explained by its name, but it is not merely an adding machine. Its function is to add the bits coming from the accumulator to those coming from main memory and produce a 1 or a 0, depending upon the components of the received bits.

Within the control unit and the arithmetic/logic unit, there are *registers*, devices which are used for temporary storage. The bits which have been taken from memory and that will be returned to memory are held in the registers.

• Memory

Perhaps the easiest way to perceive a computer's memory is to compare it with human memory.

1. There is probably a limit to the number of memory cells in the human brain, but it is generally acknowledged that that limit has never been reached. We know that only a small portion of the brain is actually used, and that with sufficient training or motivation, additional cells can be brought into use. This is demonstrated by the seemingly unlimited capacity to learn. The very fact that you are now reading a book about a subject with which you are probably unfamiliar constitutes your recognition of the existence within your brain of unused memory cells.

A computer's memory, on the other hand, is very limited indeed. Its memory cells are measurable and expressed as quantities of bytes. Thus, using the symbol K to represent 1,000, a home computer is advertised as being equipped with, for example, 4K of memory. That means it has 4,000 bytes within its memory system.

2. There seems to be no upper limit to the total amount of data that a human memory can hold. Some people seem to be able to retain more information than others and there is probably some total capacity beyond which we cannot go, but in general, training and motivation can pack ever more information into most human memories.

In a computer, on the other hand, once the "memory cells"—that is, the bytes—have been loaded with data, not a single shred of additional information can be packed into it. Each bit can hold only one unit of information, and no additional unit of information can be given to it without first removing what is already there. However, in most computer systems it is possible to add memory on to the system by hooking up additional "memory cells."

3. With the exception of the questionable skills of mind readers, there is no way to transmit the information directly from one human memory to another. Data must be removed from memory and translated into some understandable medium which may consist of words, sounds, pictures, lights, or action.

In theory—and, indeed, sometimes in practice—the fixed memory of one computer can be removed and placed in another compatible computer. It can also be transmitted from one computer to another over telephone lines.

4. The information stored in a human memory consists of both instructions and data. For example, you know how to tie a shoe, button a coat, balance a checkbook, start a car, etc. Thus, you have a great many sets of instructions in your memory. You also know the name of the president of the United States, the pronunciation of *Encyclopaedia Britannica,* and your mother's maiden name. Sometimes, what is merely data in one instance can be instructions in another. For example, knowing how to start a car is really only data until and unless you have a car to start.

In a computer, memory also consists of both data and instructions. However, they are not interchangeable as in the human memory. To a computer, an instruction is an instruction and a piece of information is a piece of information.

There are three types of computer memory; they can be thought of as main memory, long-term memory, and learned memory.

Main memory is the working memory of the computer. Necessary instructions for performing the immediate tasks at hand are taken from storage units and placed into the main memory by the control unit. Information and instructions from the input device are also placed in main memory. When all of the data

and instructions have been placed in memory, the *accumulator* (the registers that temporarily hold arithmetic and logical results in the ALU) is cleared and the computer goes to work performing its specified task.

Long-term memory is sometimes called *storage.* Its operation is generally slower than main memory and in comparison to the main, or short-term, memory, contains huge quantities of information. That information can be called into use by the control unit of the CPU as it is needed.

Learned memory is essentially a set of carefully detailed instructions that tell the computer exactly what to do. These instructions are called *routines* and are vital to the operation of the computer. If, for example, the computer is instructed to add a column of figures, it must use its learned memory to ascertain the steps required to perform this task. Learned memory is commonly known as *software,* a term which will become increasingly important to the user of a home computer. For example, the chances are excellent that you will be using your computer to work out your personal income tax. There is already available, at least for some computers, a software *program* (a set of instructions) which tells the computer exactly how to complete a Form 1040, as well as some of the more exotic schedules required by the seemingly sadistic denizens of the Internal Revenue Service. Without such software, it would be necessary for you to develop a program showing the machine how to compile the information, perform the calculations, and complete the necessary forms. With the prepackaged software, you need only feed in the specifics of your income for the machine to calculate and tell you just how much trouble you are in with the government. (We shall have more to say about software later.)

There are several types of memory, including *core, drum, disk,* and *magnetic tape.* For personal computing, however, the two most important types of memory are those on so-called "chips" and tape cassettes. Before discussing these various types, however, it will be helpful to have a somewhat clearer picture of what memory looks like. To do that, let's go through a quick review:

Within the computer, binary digits are represented by "on" or "off"—more correctly, "pulse" and "no-pulse," referring to electrical pulses. The "on" or "pulse" is a 1, the "off" or "no-pulse" is a 0. These binary digits are called *bits.* Eight of these bits are combined to form a *character,* and these characters are called *bytes.* Now, these characters, in turn, must be combined to form a *word.* A word, therefore, consists of a given number of characters or bytes; the specific number varies with the specific computer. Thus, one computer may use a two-byte word, another a four-byte word, etc. The computer treats each word as a single working unit, so when data is transported from one part of the computer to another, it is moved in the form of words.

Now let's return to our discussion of memory. Computer memory can be visualized as an array of tiny compartments. Each compartment carries a pertinent label, known as its *address.* The memory address is very similar to your own home address. Because it is always the same, anyone who *has* to know where to find your house *can* know where to find it. Similarly, because the memory address is always the same, the control unit always knows where to find it and can put into the compartment whatever must go there or take out of it whatever has been stored there.

If you are still visualizing the array of tiny compartments, then you are probably seeing them as a kind of honeycomb hanging somewhere in the air. Let's bring that image down to earth by defining a few basic terms.

Core. Core memory consists of a grid of very fine wires. Where the wires cross, minute iron rings encircle the intersection. These rings may be magnetized by the application of electrical current. When the magnetic field in one of these rings, or *cores,* runs clockwise, it represents binary digit 1; a counterclockwise magnetic field, therefore, obviously represents binary digit 0. Each point of intersection is an address. Core memory is used in large computers, and there is little likelihood of its being included in a home computer. It is mentioned because you may hear it referred to and therefore ought to know what it is, but there is no need to dwell on it further here.

Drums. A drum is a cylinder coated with material somewhat similar to the brown coating on recording tape. In operation, the drum spins past a series of electromagnets called *heads.* The heads respond to a pulse of electricity by placing a magnetic point on the drum surface. Each magnetic dot represents the binary digit 1. The absence of a dot represents a binary digit 0. If you have a tape recorder, you may have noticed that the same heads in the recorder are used for recording onto the tape as are used for playback. Similarly, when properly instructed, the heads can either "write" on or "read" from the drum.

Disks. The method here is somewhat similar to that employed for drums except, as the word suggests, the recording is done on disks that somewhat resemble a stack of phonograph records. The chief advantage of disks over drums is that the stacks can be more readily changed and substituted for other stacks. This increases the capacity for storing information.

A variation of the disk is the "floppy" disk (so called because it is flexible). Simpler technology makes the floppy disk cheaper than the metal disk used by the large computers, but it is also slower. If a home computer uses disk memory, it will almost certainly be the floppy-disk type.

Chips. In home computers, the most commonly used type of memory is the semiconductor chip. These are small, relatively inexpensive, and capable of packing monumental quantities of information into an astonishingly small space. One tenth of a square inch can often contain over four thousand bits.

We will have more to say about semiconductors and chips in Chapter 4. For this discussion, however, it is important to remember that the chief advantage of a chip is its capability of providing *random-access memory (RAM)*. To reach the little compartments—the *addresses*—in memory, it could be necessary to go through each little compartment as it occurs in sequence, extracting information whenever the wanted compartment is reached. As far as computers are concerned, such a process can be extremely slow. Large computers make it possible to randomly access data from core, drums, or disks, but that requires very complex and very expensive circuitry. The semiconductor chip, however, makes random access possible at relatively low cost and greatly increases the speed with which the equipment operates. (It has perhaps not escaped your attention that the word "access" has been used as a verb. That is pure computerese, and there is no escaping it.)

Read-Only Memory (ROM). As explained earlier, a computer must have a set of instructions to perform its functions. These sets of instructions are called *software*. By employing certain recently developed manufacturing techniques, manufacturers can permanently "engrave" these instructions onto a semiconductor chip. Inasmuch as the memory cannot be erased so that additional information or other information can then be put into it, this is known as a *read-only memory (ROM)*. ROM is not exactly *hardware*, the computer industry's term for the machine itself and all of its physical components—metal, plastic, glass, etc. Nor is it *software*, because, strictly speaking, software can be changed. Someone, therefore, devised the rather clever and appropriate designation of *firmware*. (These analogies, however, can sometimes be carried too far: at least one writer has actually referred to the

human brain as "wetware.") The book you are now reading is, in a sense, firmware: it can be removed from being accessed by the "computer" in your head and instantly become irrelevant. But the book itself cannot be changed without destroying it.

One of the chief differences between ROM and RAM is that ROM retains its input indefinitely, whereas RAM, in a home computer, will "forget" the data that has been put into it as soon as the power is turned off.

A rather elegant refinement of ROM is *erasable programmable read-only memory*, which is sometimes called EPROM, but is more commonly known as PROM. A PROM is permanent, or fixed, memory for as long as the user wishes it to be. But when the information stored in PROM is no longer needed, PROM chips can be erased by exposure to an ultraviolet light. A new program can then be stored in the PROM and will remain there until erased. An interesting variation of PROM, while somewhat sophisticated for beginners, is nevertheless worth knowing about. It is called EAROM, which stands for *electrically alterable read-only memory*. EAROM can be erased by an electrical signal. That means that although EAROM is a read-only memory, its automatic erasure can be programmed.

Cassettes. For personal computing, the tape cassette—the kind used in tape recorders—is one of the best types of memory available. It is inexpensive, and an ordinary tape recorder can be hooked up to the computer for input. The data to be stored is converted into audio tones which are then recorded on the tape. When the information is required, it is "played back" and reconverted to electrical impulses. The chief disadvantage of tape cassettes is that they cannot be randomly accessed. This means that data must be read in sequence, and sometimes a great deal of data may have to be gone through to arrive at the particular piece of information that is wanted. Retrieval, therefore, takes much longer than it would with RAM. Thus, tape cassettes are most useful when large quantities of data are to be read and processed as part of a continuing program, or when such programs need to be stored so that they can later be read into memory. When purchasing your personal computing equipment, care should be taken to see that systems using tape cassettes are supported by reasonable amounts of available software.

There is another advantage to tape cassettes, one that is shared by floppy disks and some other types of memory: it is memory which is transferable. If I record a message on my tape recorder, remove the cassette and mail the cassette to you, you can place that cassette in your tape recorder and receive that message—always provided, of course, that we speak the same language. The same holds true for computers. As long as the equipment can accept the memory, and as long as the computers speak the same language, then, in effect, computers can "talk" to each other.

While that is an important and interesting concept, it is more important that computers communicate with the people using them. All of that arithmetic, logic, calculating, comparing—in short, *data processing*—going on inside the central processing unit is of little value until and unless the computer can tell us what is going on and what it knows.

3

THE COMPUTER SPEAKS

We have been talking at some length about giving instructions and information to a computer. We have also discussed what the computer can tell us. But how is this information conveyed to and from that electronic wonder? As already mentioned, this communication with the computer is done through input/output (I/O) devices.

Sophisticated computer systems often use some rather exotic input devices, sometimes consisting of a complexity of electronic circuitry that can perform such minor miracles as transforming the configurations of the human body into bits and bytes.

• I/O Ports

A port is a kind of staging area. Data from an input device passes through the port and is processed for use by the computer. Similarly, the computer's output first passes through the port, where it is prepared for the output device. In home computers, most ports are used for both input and output and are, therefore, called I/O ports.

There are two kinds of I/O ports. The *serial* port receives data serially—that is, one bit at a time—and feeds it into the computer that way. Processed data is returned to the output device in the same way—one bit at a time. Continuing efforts to reduce the processing time have led to the development of the *parallel* port, which is capable of handling considerable quantities of data at one time.

This parallel input and output of data is performed by a group of electrical conductors capable of carrying several electronic impulses simultaneously, usually to different parts of the computer. This arrangement is called a *bus*. The electrical conductors can be wires or copper traces, but in home computers, they are likely to consist of a printed circuit board. Buses are used for a number of functions within the computer. Where several buses are used together, it is called a *bus system*. The parallel I/O port consists of a data bus plus the so-called *"handshake"* signal, which establishes synchronization between the I/O device and the central processing unit.

At this point, it is probably useful to introduce the word *peripheral*. The word is used as both a noun and an adjective. For example,

Radio Shack's complete, self-contained, ready-to-plug-in system. Clockwise from twelve o'clock are the CRT display, the power supply, a tape cassette recorder/player, and keyboard. Courtesy Radio Shack.

the tape recorder that is used to transfer data from the cassette to the computer is outside of —that is, peripheral to—the computer. It is, therefore, correctly called a peripheral. Later on in this book, we will review the advantages and disadvantages of purchasing a complete, self-contained home computer or building your own. For now, remember that if you buy a self-contained unit, the I/O devices will be an integral part of that unit (although it may be designed to accept some peripherals).

• Input

The input device most commonly used with a personal computer is a keyboard. If you have a push-button telephone, then you are already acquainted with one type of keyboard that is often used. Such keyboards permit the entry not only of data but of programs. But as is immediately obvious, it is limited only to entries made by digits and a few symbols. (A hand-held calculator has a similar keyboard.) Such keyboards are always used together with a display so that the operator can check on the entries as they are being made. Frequently, this type of keyboard is called a *keypad,* to distinguish it from typewriter-like keyboards.

By far the most common type of keyboard is one that resembles a typewriter. This permits the entry of data and instructions through the use of words and letters. This keyboard is also usually hooked up to some sort of display so that the data can be viewed as it is being entered. That display will also be used for the output, which is why input/output devices are generally discussed as a unit.

If you are electronically inclined, you might want to look around for a used Teletype machine. The Teletypewriter has a long and distinguished history as an I/O device. Any number of variations are available from used-equipment dealers. The electronics involved in Teletypewriter circuitry are, by comparision to other I/O devices, inexpensive and easy to deal with, which makes the machine a particular favorite among computer hobbyists. (The mechanics of a Teletypewriter, however, are complicated, with hundreds of moving parts.) Among the types available are the "receive only (RO)" which is really an output device because it has no keyboard and can be used only as a printer. "Key, send, and receive (KSR)" models not only provide a print-out, but also enable the operator to key data into the computer. If you are not already overwhelmed by initials and acronyms, try to remember that when you hear a computer enthusiast referring to a "TTY," he means a Teletypewriter.

If you have looked at some personal computers, particularly one that has been put together by a hobbyist, you may have noticed that on the computer's front panel there are a number of switches. These switches provide for the entry of data, literally on a bit-by-bit basis, by turning a series of those switches on or off. This is known as *binary key input.* It

usually comes as part of a kit, along with instructions for its construction and use. Its chief advantage is its low cost: it is probably cheaper than just about any other input method. Whether the saving is worth the trouble can only be determined by the user's interest in electronics, desire for and affinity toward putting things together, and willingness to spend a lot of time with a hot soldering iron.

• Output

There are several types of output devices. Most people have some familiarity with all of them: video displays, printers, and audio devices.

Video displays. Perhaps the most popular device for home computers—particularly those that are self-contained, ready-to-use systems that need only be purchased, taken home and plugged in—are the display terminals that look like television screens. A TV screen is actually the visible surface of a large and complicated piece of electronic apparatus known as a *cathode ray tube (CRT),* and it is this same tube that is used for the video displays that are hooked up to computers. They are, therefore, commonly known as CRT terminals or CRT I/O devices—or simply, CRTs.

The chief advantage of the video display terminal is its dual function as an I/O device. It not only displays input as it is being put in; it also provides the read-out for the computer's output.

If you purchase a home computer system that does not come with a video display terminal, there are several ways of adding one on. The simplest is to purchase a terminal that comes equipped with a keyboard. As the data is keyed on the keyboard, it is displayed on the screen. When the user determines that the information displayed on the screen is correct, the appropriate key is pressed and the computer begins processing the data. Computer hobbyists who enjoy putting things together can, of course, purchase CRT terminals and keyboards separately and perform the necessary electrical hookups so that they function with the computer and each other. Complete terminals are also available in kit form.

Many computers are hooked up to a *video monitor*. If you have ever visited a TV studio, you have probably seen monitors in operation. The monitor is the TV set that shows what is going out "over the air" from the studio; it cannot receive signals from other TV stations. Computer hobby stores usually have a wide variety of video monitors, including second-hand ones, available in a broad range of prices.

If you become addicted to tinkering with electronics, or if you know someone who is a *bona fide* expert in such things, you may want to convert a conventional television set for use as a CRT terminal. Such conversion requires not only skill, but faith, as the slightest mistake can result in shock and even electrocution. Considerable damage can also be done to the computer.

Many computer hobby stores and mail-order firms sell an *RF* (for "radio frequency") *converter*, which enables the user to hook up a conventional TV set to the computer. The RF converter works through the TV set's antenna terminals. If you choose to purchase such a device—or a kit for constructing one—make certain that the one you buy has been approved by the Federal Communications Commission. You may have to search far and wide for one that has such approval. Unapproved RF converters often interfere with nearby TV reception, incurring the enmity of one's neighbors.

Also available are color video terminals. Such terminals can be built by the enthusiast, or, with an FCC-approved RF converter, the home color TV set can be connected to the computer. Several *interfaces* (that is, devices that enable the computer to be hooked up to a color TV) are available. They are expensive and, apart from their game-playing and dubious esthetic qualities, there seems to be little real need for color TV terminals—except, perhaps, in some highly specialized applications.

Almost every major department store and many toy and game dealers now have electronic games, constructed around miniature computers, that can be easily hooked up to a home television. The hookup usually requires no more than a screwdriver and the ability to read some simple instructions. In such configurations, the home TV set can be considered a peripheral to the computer locked up inside the game. Some TV manufacturers have now begun marketing new models which contain jacks or plugs so that the TV games can simply be plugged in. It is only a matter of time—and very little time, at that—until those jacks and plugs will be able to accommodate an *interface* (the adapter which makes two separate pieces of equipment work together) with which you can literally plug your computer into your TV set.

Perhaps the chief disadvantage of a video display terminal is its inability to render a permanent record of what it displays. In computer parlance, such a permanent record is called *hard copy*. (A *print-out* is one form of hard copy.) One of the more ingenious methods for obtaining hard copy from a video display terminal is to attach a Polaroid camera to the terminal by means of a bracket. It will not require much in the way of mechanics to arrange the camera so that it can swing out of the way when not in use, and when needed, can be placed in position so that it is the right distance from the screen to include the entire screen in the picture. The camera can also be set at a permanent-focus position. The computer user can then obtain hard copy by taking a Polaroid picture of the video screen.

There are, however somewhat more efficient and more legible ways of obtaining hard copy.

• Printers

As mentioned earlier, the Teletypewriter (TTY) can be used as both an input and an output device that will render hard copy.

An excellent and versatile output printer is an IBM Selectric typewriter. Some Selectric models are equipped to hook up directly to computers, but these are quite expensive. Most computer stores and many mail-order companies supply devices or kits which can transform a standard Selectric typewriter into a computer peripheral that can be simply plugged in. And, of course, when not sending messages to or receiving replies from a computer, a Selectric typewriter functions as a typewriter.

If you have ever had the opportunity to visit the computer room in a commercial installation, you probably gazed open-mouthed at the printers regurgitating yards of paper upon which thousands of characters have been impressed in the blink of an eye. It would be pointless and probably prohibitively expensive to attempt to attach such a printer to a home computer. But smaller versions are available. One manufacturer offers a printer that uses adding-machine paper and pounds out a respectable 110 characters per second.

• Punched Tape I/O Devices

Prior to the advent of computers, certain Teletypewriters utilized punched paper tape for feeding information into and out of the machinery. That could account for the popularity of paper tape I/O devices in the early days of microcomputers: the TTYs were available as I/Os.

There is more than one tape system, but typically a punched tape is made of paper or mylar about an inch wide. Sprocket holes are punched down its middle for guiding the tape. Data is stored on the tape by punching a series of holes into it. There are eight vertical positions on the tape where data may be punched. These positions are known as *channels*. (One system uses only five channels.) The pattern in which these positions are punched or not punched comprises a code that represents a character. (Generally, the ASCII code is used.)

The tape is placed into a tape guide and passes over a series of thin metal electrical contacts. When a hole permits a contact to penetrate, a circuit is closed, causing a signal to be generated. The combinations that these contacts make form the word that is typed out on the TTY or fed into the computer (depending on whether the device is being used for input or output). With some tape readers, the tape itself is usually guided through manually and the operator pulls the tape as slowly or as quickly as he desires, but not so fast that he is racing ahead of his computer's capacity. An obvious danger here is that paper tape can be torn by an enthusiastic operator.

Some tape readers use an optical system involving photosensitive cells, but optical tape readers are expensive (although there is one model carried by many computer stores that is somewhat lower in cost than the commercial ones).

The chief disadvantages of punched tape are slowness and space. Rigid-disk memory operates at a rate of more than a million characters per second. Floppy-disk memory runs at anywhere between a thousand and ten thousand characters per second. Tape cassettes, considered by advanced computer hobbyists to be slow, can be read or written to at anywhere from thirty to a thousand characters per second. Reading and writing with paper tape can run from ten to a hundred characters per second. As for storage space, it requires over six hundred yards of paper tape to record the same quantity of information that can be stored on one C-90 tape cassette. The prosecution rests.

● **Audio Peripherals**

When you dial a telephone to get the correct time or when a voice comes on to inform you that you have reached a wrong number, what you are hearing is a computerized voice simulator. Extensive research is now going on to develop computer systems that can "hear" the human voice and receive input that way, but voice-simulated output is already well developed. There are at least two voice simulators on the market designed for use with home computers. They are expensive—in the $400 range—but prices will probably come down eventually.

Music, on the other hand, is quite another story. There are currently available various peripherals that emit musical tones, and these are relatively low-priced. By programming the computer properly, music—or at least what purports to be music—can be performed by the computer. We shall have more to say on this subject in Chapter 9, "Fun and Games."

In a certain sense, a home computer can be compared with a camera. The technically skilled amateur photographer can begin with a basic camera body around which he can construct a system of photography with almost unlimited capabilities. He can buy telephoto lenses, wide-angle lenses, microscope at-

tachments, lighting equipment of varying types, special viewfinders, dozens of filters, testing and checking equipment, motor drives, cable releases, and all kinds of other equipment, attachments, and accessories. The less skilled photographer may prefer a camera for which equipment, attachments, and accessories are fewer in number but which are essentially easier to operate. He may prefer buying self-contained units—such as an electronic flash gun—which can be quickly and easily hooked up to the camera. And finally, there are perhaps millions of photographers content with an Instamatic, a cartridge of film, and a pocket full of flash cubes.

Because of the relative newness of the field, in terms of quantity and sophistication, home computers perhaps offer somewhat less for hobbyists than does the photographic industry. Nevertheless, a wide variety of peripherals and other additions and accessories are available to the computer hobbyist. For example, it is not difficult for a computer hobbyist to begin with a basic 4K memory computer and gradually build that up to a system with 8K, 12K, or 16K and even more memory.

Similarly, there are people who are not interested in the intricacies of electronics and who, at best, might be prepared to assemble a simple kit, but who really would prefer "add-ons" that need only be plugged into their home computers. Again, many such add-ons are either available now or will be in the very near future.

The decision as to which path to take must, of course, rest with you. There are two things to be careful about:

First, before you buy any peripheral—be it kit, finished product, or a boxful of wires, plugs, and printed circuits—make certain that what you are purchasing is compatible with the computer you have in your home. Not every video display terminal with a keyboard can be used with every computer.

Second, be certain that the peripheral or accessory that you are buying will perform the job that you want it to, in accordance with your needs. It may be moderately amusing, at least at first, to have a Teletypewriter clacking away in your living room at the push of a button, but if you do not need hard copy, and if the clacking is keeping the baby awake, then the TTY may prove to be an error in judgment.

Remember the injunction of the first sentence of the first chapter of this book: computers, unless they are broken, never make mistakes. People, however, frequently do.

4
MICROPROCESSORS

In the late 1950s, researchers at Bell Laboratories developed the transistor, which virtually replaced the old-fashioned vacuum tube. Because of its tiny size, the transistor opened doorways in many areas of electronics that led to miniaturization and, eventually, to subminiaturization. With the advent of the transistor, for example, it became possible to manufacture hearing aids that could be placed directly inside the ear and be virtually invisible. Radios of fairly good range and passable tonal quality could be—and are—made small enough to slip into a shirt pocket.

A further development of the transistor is *"large-scale integration"* (*LSI*), a process which allows for the arrangement of thousands of nearly microscopic transistors, forming an integrated circuit, on a minuscule slice of silicon. Silicon is a nonmetallic element that is found in the earth's crust. Its chief advantages, from an electronics point of view, are its purity and its function as a *semiconductor*.

If you remember your high school science, then you know that certain materials, such as copper, carry or "conduct" electricity very well, while other materials, such as rubber or wood, do not conduct electricity at all and are therefore used for insulation against electrical flow. As the term implies, a semiconductor lies somewhere in between. It is neither a particularly good nor a particularly bad conductor. But the "neutrality" of a semiconductor can be altered by implanting certain "impurities," such as atoms of phosphorus or arsenic. This makes possible the introduction of positive and negative charges, which in turn make it possible to implant transistors. (Exactly how this is done is explained in detail in virtually any decent general science text, such as *Asimov's Guide to Science,* published by Basic Books, and the *Penguin Dictionary of Science,* published by Schocken. Incidentally, although silicon is the one most often used in computers, it is not the only semiconductor; germanium is also well-known and widely used in other applications.)

In the mid-1960s computer technologists developed a method for etching circuitry and logic functions onto a small chip of silicon. A master drawing, about five hundred times larger than the actual chip, is photographically reduced to the required size. Then, employing a method which is very like photoengraving, the minuscule photograph of the drawing is etched onto the chip. As a result of this circuitry-on-a-chip technique, manufacturers were able to considerably reduce both the cost and the size of computers,

Surrounded by contact lenses to show relative size,
this tiny chip of silicon, approximately one-twentieth
of an inch square, contains a central processing unit
(CPU). Courtesy Texas Instruments.

giving rise to a new subindustry: minicomputers. Chip technology also made it possible to produce small personal "computers" with fixed, nonalterable programs. Hand-held calculators and electronic digital watches are examples of these personal computers.

In 1969, M. E. Hoff, Jr., an engineer for Intel Corporation, a manufacturer of logic and circuitry chips, was placed in charge of a project to produce calculator chips for Busicom, a Japanese company manufacturing calculators. While searching for an economical method of meeting the customer's needs, Mr. Hoff discovered that he could incorporate the entire central processing unit on a single silicon chip. By attaching two additional chips— one for input and output of data and another for inscribing a program—Mr. Hoff had what amounted to a basic computer. By the time Intel's engineering team worked over Mr. Hoff's invention, it contained 2,250 transistors on a chip that was just under a sixth of an inch in length and an eighth of an inch wide. Each of these transistors was approximately equal to one of the vacuum tubes in the pioneering ENIAC computer. Interestingly, this *microcomputer,* as it was known, could be mass-produced on the same production lines on

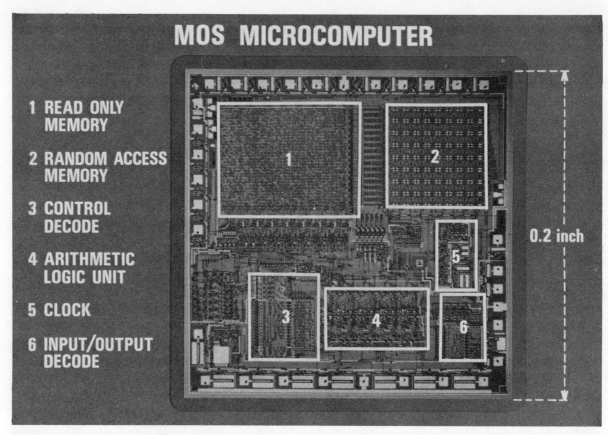

MOS MICROCOMPUTER

1 READ ONLY MEMORY

2 RANDOM ACCESS MEMORY

3 CONTROL DECODE

4 ARITHMETIC LOGIC UNIT

5 CLOCK

6 INPUT/OUTPUT DECODE

0.2 inch

A close-up of a microcomputer on a chip. Courtesy Texas Instruments.

which Intel made their memory chips. As a result, the company was now in the business of manufacturing computers.

Micro derives from the Greek word *mikros,* meaning small. (It is often designated by the Greek letter *mu* and written in Greek like this: μ.) The central processing unit (CPU) in a microcomputer is generally referred to as an MPU—a microprocessing unit. Up to now we have been using the terms "home computer" or "personal computer." From now on, we will refer only to microcomputers because that is what home and personal computers are.

Chips and various other components were mounted on boards made of plastic, known as *printed circuit boards.* The interconnections, consisting of etched foil, or plated conducting pads, were rigid and unalterable. They contained the program and became known as *"hard-wired logic."* The typical hand-held calculator (other than the programmable models) is an example of hard-wired logic. The operating program instructions, which consist of the arithmetic functions, are etched permanently in the chips. The application program is, in effect, in the operator's brain. He provides the instructions for performing the specific calculations that achieve the desired results.

Although microprocessors got off to a rather slow start, by the mid-1970s they began to appear everywhere. Among automobile manufacturers, General Motors announced that a microcomputer would be used in its 1977 Oldsmobile Coronado to improve fuel economy by controlling sparkplug firing. Cadillac offers its owners a "trip-master" which computes the driver's estimated arrival time and other useful information. The 1978 Ford Versailles came equipped with microcomputers.

In the meantime, microprocessors are showing up in a wide variety of products. Singer Sewing Machine's Athena 2000 uses an MPU to eliminate some 350 parts that normally go into sewing machines, while at the same time allowing the operator to produce any one of two dozen different stitch patterns. Amana, in its Touchmatic Micro Wave Oven, was the first to use a microprocessor in such a device. Other companies quickly followed suit. MPUs are showing up in scanning radio receivers, self-service gas pumps, coin-operated machines that can take your blood pressure, digital clocks and watches, "talking" calculators for the blind, laboratory testing equipment, drink dispensers in bars, etc. In the planning stages—and possibly even on the market by the time you read this—are refrigerators, clothes washers and dryers, dishwashers, home temperature controls, and dozens of other household products equipped with microprocessors. Those products will be cheaper to maintain because they will have fewer moving parts, and they will be cheaper to operate because they will make the most efficient use of energy.

In the meantime, many people are having a lot of fun with MPUs. Electronic games which can be easily plugged into home television sets are being sold almost faster than manufacturers can produce them. The MPUs also provide many hours of diversion and amusement for a new species, which, if not native to America, certainly flourishes here: the computer hobbyist. Thanks to the MPU, it is possible to construct a highly sophisticated, reliable, and versatile computer for relatively little money. Perhaps even more interesting, the MPU has made it possible for companies to manufacture and market complete, self-contained, ready-to-plug-in-and-go computers at prices well within the range of the average middle-class American.

The microcomputer *is* the home computer.

5

THE HOME COMPUTER—BASIC COMPONENTS

So far we've been talking, somewhat non-specifically, about various components of computers. We know, for example, that to be regarded as a computer, a system must consist of a central processing unit, memory, and input/output devices. That holds true whether the computer is housed in a collection of formidable-looking steel boxes that occupy half a floor over at corporate headquarters, or whether the computer is located on a couple of chips of silicon and gives you the time of day or helps you balance your checkbook. Now let's get down to specifics and see what precisely ought to be included in your personal computer.

The microprocessor. Contained in one or several integrated circuit chips, it carries the arithmetic/logic unit (ALU), the controls required to operate the computer, and the working registers. (A *register,* you will recall, is a temporary storage location for data.)

Memory. In all likelihood, the printed circuit board (sometimes called *card*) that holds the microprocessing unit (MPU: synonymous in home computers with CPU) will also hold some memory. More memory can be added on in almost every case, either by means of additional printed circuit boards or one of several peripheral memory devices.

Clock. This is a new term which the novice ought to know about, although involvement with it depends to a great extent upon whether you are building a system yourself or buying a complete unit. The clock in a computer creates high-frequency oscillations that are controlled by a crystal (similar in principle to the quartz crystal in a digital watch). Its function is to provide carefully controlled electric pulses at predetermined intervals, so that all of the components of the microcomputer are marching to the same beat. (Incidentally, the speed with which a computer operates generally governs the cost of a unit. It is not unusual for a microcomputer to perform program operations at the rate of about 500,000 a second, give or take a few beats.)

Data input device. Almost certainly, this will consist of some sort of keyboard. In a system that the operator has put together from scratch, the keyboard may be a separately purchased mechanism—perhaps from an obsolete terminal—that has been wired into the system. More likely, however, for beginners the keyboard will be part of a video display terminal or an electric typewriter which has a built-in interface so that it can be hooked up to the computer system. Or, it will be one that can be connected to the microcomputer through relatively easy-to-obtain and easy-to-use adapters.

Output device. This is likely to be a video display or some form of printer—e.g. a typewriter or Teletypewriter.

Power supply. Strictly speaking, the power supply is the wall socket into which you plug your computer. However, most home computers operate on direct current (DC), while most household electricity is alternating current (AC). The power supply in a microcomputer system converts the current from AC to DC and maintains a steady, consistent, nonfluctuating flow of electricity. In a microcomputer the power supply may have to provide varying voltages for different functions.

If you own a calculator, a transistor radio, or a tape recorder that operates on batteries and have a so-called "AC adapter," then you have some idea of the power supply's function. A typical AC adapter converts 120 volts of alternating current to six volts of direct current. The power supply in a microcomputer performs essentially the same function. Most of the time, the power supply is an integral part of the microcomputer's system, but sometimes prices for such computers do not include the cost of the power supply. It is worth making sure that a power supply is either included in the price, or the price for it is given so that you can add it to the total cost. It is possible to make your own power supply, but some training in electronics plus previous experience in putting electrical devices together are prerequisites. If you must build, there are kits available at computer hobby stories.

Software. This consists primarily of the programs used to obtain a particular result through a set of sequential instructions or statements given to the computer. Programs and programming will be discussed at greater length in Chapters 7 and 8.

Cabinets. For once, here is a singularly untechnical term that means exactly what you think it means. It is not unusual for a computer hobbyist to show off his system as what appears to be a bristling array of wires, boards, transistors, resistors, a partly disassembled typewriter, etc. In the interests of both esthetics and careful maintenance, however, it is usually better to enclose the system in some kind of box. It not only looks better, but it keeps out dust and inquisitive fingers. Even if you decide to construct a computer from a kit or from individually purchased components, chances are that some sort of case, cover, or cabinet is available. Buy it.

These are the basic components for every microcomputer system. There are, of course, other devices and facilities which can be added on. Also, almost all of the components listed above are in themselves complex arrangements of electronic circuitry. Thus, each part may itself consist of many parts.

For example, don't forget the *bus,* the system of wires that transmits data or addresses from one part of the microcomputer to another. The data is offered to all of the parts that are connected to the particular bus. Whether those parts accept all, none, or some of that data depends on whether they need it.

If there are a large number of I/O devices on the bus line, the movement of data may be slowed down, upsetting the synchronization between the various components of the computer and ultimately causing the system to malfunction. To avoid such an eventuality, a special amplifier circuit is added to the bus system. This circuit drives the I/O devices that are connected to the bus system. By now, you should be prepared for the fact that such an amplifier circuit is called a *bus driver.*

You may remember—but let's review it, anyway—that within the central processing unit (CPU) is the *control unit.* The control unit receives instructions from the program and, one by one, extracts the appropriate bits from the storage "compartments" in memory. Each instruction is decoded by the control unit or converted from its numeric representation into an appropriate electronic signal. These signals are then routed to other locations within the microprocessor. The actual work of the microcomputer is performed in other parts of the system which have received instructions from the control unit as to what data to work on and how and when to do it.

Also located in the CPU is the *arithmetic/ logic unit* (ALU). Here is where the actual computation—that is, the arithmetic functions —is performed.

The *accumulator* is part of the ALU. It consists of a register in which the arithmetic and logical results are temporarily stored. It is analogous to a chalkboard where sums and other results are temporarily written down and saved until they are needed, at which time they can be erased.

There are, as you may well imagine, hundreds of other terms applicable to computers that describe devices, electronic circuitry, and functions. Some apply to computers in general, others specifically to microcomputers. Most of the important ones are given in the Glossary beginning on page 94. How many of these you will be required to know depends entirely on how intimately you plan to become involved with the nuts and bolts of your computing equipment.

But whether you buy a system or build one, whether you are totally ignorant of its inner workings or thoroughly cognizant of every switch and pulse, when you turn your computer on, it will do nothing but hum at you.

It is waiting for you to talk to it.

6

SPEAKING YOUR COMPUTER'S LANGUAGE

All computers, regardless of size, capacity, cost, function, simplicity, complexity, or utility, have one thing in common: way down deep inside the bowels of the machine, where all the work is done, electrical pulses are being turned on or off. A pulse represents binary digit 1; a no-pulse represents binary digit 0. All information that is fed into the computer, whether operating instructions or data, ultimately must be reduced to the pulse/no-pulse "language" of the computer.

At first, the only way computers could be programmed was to write the program using a series of binary numbers. (A *program,* you may recall, is a list of instructions or statements, written in sequence, that will result in the computer's performance of a particular function or task.) Understandably, people who could do such things were regarded with awe and reverence, intermingled with a little suspicion. The opportunity for error was enormous.

Before long, it was realized that if a computer could be programmed to perform certain functions, then one of those functions could be the translation from a less complicated (to humans) language into the binary lingo of the machine. The result of that inspiration was *assembly language,* and programs

called *assemblers.* Assembly language consists of *mnemonics,* made up of combinations of letters. Each mnemonic represents a computer instruction. The assembler program translates the assembly language into the binary number system for the computer.

It was only a relatively short step to the development of so-called *high-level languages.* Some of these languages come very close to plain English. Among the more popular are *COBOL* (an acronym for *Co*mmon *Bu*siness-*O*riented *L*anguage), a language that requires only a perfunctory familiarity with the internal workings of a computer. If the programmer understands the rules involved in organizing a COBOL program, he can write such a program with little difficulty and, with some adjustments, it will run on any computer equipped with a COBOL compiler. (More about compilers shortly.) *FORTRAN* (an acronym for *For*mula *Tra*nslator) is a computer language used primarily for scientific and mathematical purposes. Mathematical symbols and formulas make up the foundation of FORTRAN and enable the programmer to write a complicated mathematics problem with only a few instructions.

Another common language is *BASIC* (an acronym for *B*eginner's *A*ll-Purpose *S*ymbolic

*I*nstruction *C*ode). This language was initially developed for use by students, but it has been improved and expanded. Virtually every home computer is equipped for programming in BASIC, and we'll have a good deal more to say about this language later on.

Just as the assembly language is processed through an assembler program, the high-level languages are processed through a program called a *compiler*. It may be convenient to think of assemblers and compilers as being essentially the same thing. The main differences are that the assembler, of course, deals with assembly language and the compiler deals with a high-level language. The most important difference, however, is that, because assembly language is closer to *machine language* (that is, the binary-number language of the computer), the assembler has many fewer steps to reduce the language of the programmer to the language of the machine and is, therefore, a faster program than the compiler. (It is important to bear in mind, however, that when we talk about speed in a computer, we are talking about measurements in *microseconds* [one millionth of a second] and even *nanoseconds* [one billionth of a second].)

A program that is written in a form that is directly readable by the computer is called an *object program*. A program written in a higher-level language is called a *source program*. The computer translates the source program into an object program before it begins working on the set of instructions.

Most home computers use a special compiler program called an *interpreter*. The compiler converts all of the source program's instructions to machine language and then, in effect, steps aside, freeing up memory for other uses. The interpreter, however, converts an instruction, waits for the CPU to implement that instruction, then converts the next instruction, and so on. The interpreter, then, must remain in memory until the entire source program is completed. While this ties up some

of the memory, it is worth the price, because the interpreter permits quick changes in instructions, which the usual kind of compiler does not. With most systems, the sacrifice of memory can be easily compensated for by relatively inexpensive add-on memory. (For technical reasons too complicated and boring to go into here, interpreters work most efficiently with BASIC, less so with more complicated languages.)

BASIC is, beyond question, the most commonly used language for microcomputers. Its appeal is obvious: it is almost identical to English. A raw beginner with a reasonable amount of intelligence can learn to do programming in BASIC with the aid of one or two books and three or four evenings of quiet study and practice.

There are a number of versions of BASIC, including Extended BASIC, BASIC, Tiny BASIC and Micro BASIC. These vary in versatility and in the cost of the hardware that is required to handle them—Extended BASIC being the most sophisticated, and Micro BASIC the simplest. Different versions of BASIC exist because, unfortunately (at least at this writing), there is no standard for BASIC. As a result, each manufacturer uses a version of the language that differs somewhat from that of other manufacturers. For that reason, it is impossible to include in this book a course of study in BASIC or even to recommend a course of study. The form of BASIC you learn will depend on the particular machine you own. But these variations should prove to be little more than a minor annoyance; when you have learned BASIC for one machine, you will have little difficulty in learning it for another.

Even within the variations there are variations. Tiny BASIC, for example, a language originally developed by People's Computer Company, a periodical publisher, enjoyed immediate success and was used for a number of computers before some standardization could be established. (As a result, even Tiny BASIC varies from one computer to another.) The designation "tiny" derives from the fact that one need learn relatively little in order to write programs in the language, and the computer that uses Tiny BASIC is comparatively small, and so is its cost.

Various versions of BASIC are constantly being developed, improved, refined, and expended. Microcomputer owners who want to know more about BASIC, not only for cultural enhancement but to increase the versatility of their computer use, would do well to subscribe to one of the computer hobby publications mentioned in the Bibliography.

The microcomputer you buy should come equipped with a manual that includes, among other things, some of the basics of BASIC. It will take a very short time to master the manual. Then a visit to a computer store or review of publications available by mail will easily and quickly provide you with a more detailed study program for learning the version of BASIC needed for your computer.

7

PROGRAMMING

• What a Program Is

As you now know, probably to the point of boredom, a program is a set of instructions by which a computer performs certain functions or delivers a desired result. The implication is that programming applies only to computers and that it involves very complicated problems and procedures. But as a matter of fact, a program can involve working merely with pencil and paper and solving a fairly simple problem. Indeed, when regarded at its most basic level, a computer is really nothing more than a high-speed electronic pencil and paper.

Let's consider the kind of problem that you will find in a junior high school student's math book but also the sort that is likely to arise in virtually any household. We'll assume that we have a room that is nine feet wide by twelve feet long and that the room is desperately in need of carpeting. In this morning's newspaper, we have seen an advertisement for exactly the kind of carpeting we need. It is priced at $12.88 per square yard and, this week only, there is a 25 per cent reduction on all the carpeting that that particular store is selling. Let's list the data that we have:

1. The room is 9 feet by 12 feet.
2. The carpeting costs $12.88 per square yard.

3. The actual price will be reduced by 25 per cent.
4. In our area, we must add a sales tax of 6 per cent.
5. There is a delivery charge of $15.

In order to determine the total cost of the carpet, we have to perform the following tasks:

1. We must calculate the total number of square yards needed for our room. (Alternatively, we could break down the price per square yard to a price per square foot, but that would make our job unnecessarily more complicated.)
2. We must calculate the price by multiplying the number of square yards we need by the price per square yard.
3. We must determine the net cost by deducting 25 per cent from the total arrived at in Step 2.
4. We must add the sales tax to the result obtained in Step 3.
5. We must add the delivery charge to the total arrived at in Step 4.

If you enjoy wasting time playing with numbers of this sort, you can work out this problem with pencil and paper in a few minutes. I prefer to use a simple hand-held calculator which has five functions: addition, subtraction, multiplication, division, and per cent calculation. Calculator in hand, we perform the following steps:

1. We multiply 9 by 12 which gives us 108 square feet.

2. Not unlike a computer, we have stored in our memory the information that there are nine square feet to the square yard, so we divide 108 square feet by 9 square feet to give us 12 square yards.

3. We now multiply 12 square yards by the price of $12.88 for a total price of $154.56.

4. We must now deduct 25 per cent of $154.56. There are several ways we can do that, but with our hand-held calculator, all we need to do is key in $154.56, press the MINUS key to show that a subtraction will follow, and then key in the numbers 2 and 5, press the PER CENT key (our read-out shows that the deduction will be $38.64), press the EQUAL key and arrive at a net total of $115.92.

5. The next step is really a reverse of Step 4 and with somewhat different numbers. We key in the result of Step 4, which is $115.92, press the PLUS key to show that an amount is to be added, press the 6 key for the sales tax, press the PER CENT key (the readout shows that $6.9552 is about to be added to the total), press the EQUAL key and arrive at a total of $122.8752, which is rounded off to $122.88.

6. We now add to $122.88 the delivery charge of $15 and we discover that the total cost of our carpet, delivered, will be $137.88.

In effect, what we have done is, first, written a program and, second, carried it out. To be sure, there are some basic flaws in our example. For one thing, it is very much of an oversimplification. For another, while our "computer" performed many of the tasks necessary in arriving at a result, particularly the most tedious, the most time-consuming, and the ones most subject to error, nevertheless, a considerable amount of human participation was involved. If we were dealing with a computer,

we would simply inform the machine to perform the following tasks:

1. Calculate square yards.
2. Calculate price for entire room.
3. Deduct discounts.
4. Add sales tax.
5. Add delivery charge.
6. Print out net result.

Of course, the data necessary to perform those calculations would also have to be entered into the machine.

The primary purpose of this overly simple and admittedly less-than-fascinating exercise is to demonstrate what has been stated previously: the computer works only in sequence. Properly programmed, a computer could deliver up that final figure of $137.88 with such speed as to seem instantaneous, but the fact is that a machine can perform only one step at a time, proceeding to each succeeding step in strict accordance with the pattern that has been predetermined by the programmer. A program can be stored in a computer, so the machine can follow the same set of instructions over and over again unless and until those instructions are erased by some other program. This is called *looping,* a process which brings the computer back to the beginning of a set of instructions, ready to repeat them as required.

● **Flowcharts**

Before beginning a program, you must know three things: (1) You must know what kind of information, or *data,* will be input; (2) you must know what data you want the machine to output; (3) you must know what steps the computer must go through to solve the problem at hand.

The easiest and most efficient way to determine the procedures that you want the computer to follow is to block out those procedures in a diagram. This diagram is called a

49

flowchart (also referred to as a block diagram, flow diagram, and logic diagram). In effect, the flowchart is a kind of map of the program that is to be written.

On page 51 is an example of a flowchart that has been circulating among computer people for many years. It shows the steps to be taken by the resident breadwinner in getting up and going to work. Designed in the antediluvian days before Women's Liberation, this flowchart makes certain assumptions which today might be considered male-chauvinistic. Nevertheless, sociology aside, it is a good example of what a flowchart looks like. You will note an inset in the upper-right portion of the flowchart; it is a very broad diagram of what has to be done, and it is hardly an adequate one. It is, however, as good a starting point as any, one from which the various refinements can be extrapolated.

The figures shown in the diagram are standard. The rectangle represents the processing step. The diamond shape signifies a decision point. All of the symbols used in a flowchart have been standardized and some of the more common ones are shown on page 52. These were drawn with the aid of a *template,* a plastic stencil readily available at computer hobby shops and large commercial stationers.

• Using a Flowchart

A computer, as we said at the outset, does more than compute; it is also capable of making decisions. To be more precise, the user tells the computer what kind of decision it wants. The computer then "decides" by making comparisons. Let's consider a specific example and go back to our carpeting problem. Having determined the cost of our carpet earlier in this chapter, we continue leafing through the newspaper only to discover that this is National Carpet Sales Week and all sorts of carpet retailers are offering all kinds

of deals. We now find ourselves confronted with several choices:

1. There is the original offer of carpeting at $12.88 a square yard, less 25 per cent discount, plus 6 per cent sales tax and a $15 delivery charge.

2. Another store is offering comparable carpeting at $13 a square yard. The price includes the sales tax and delivery.

3. A third retailer is offering carpeting at $15 a square yard, with a one-third discount, plus the same 6 per cent sales tax and $15 delivery charge.

4. And a fourth retailer is offering carpeting at $20 a square yard, plus a 6 per cent sales tax and a $15 delivery charge. This higher-priced carpeting, however, is better quality and is expected to last about fifteen years, whereas the carpeting being offered by the other three stores is expected to last about ten years.

The question we want our computer to answer is: "Which of the four deals offers the best value? Which carpet should we buy? With pencil, paper, and patience, the problem is a tedious one, but not a difficult one. We need merely calculate the cost of carpeting for a nine-by-twelve room based on each of the given prices, taking into account the various discounts, the sales tax, and the delivery charge. Once we know that, we divide the net cost of each of the first three offers by ten to give us the cost per square yard per year. We do the same for offer No. 4, except that we divide by fifteen to give us the cost per square yard per year. Faced with this kind of pencil-and-paper computation, the prospect of having a computer do all this dirty work has a certain undeniable appeal. As a matter of fact, it would probably be a lot easier to work this problem with pencil, paper, and a hand-held calculator, because that would probably take less time than drawing a flowchart and then writing a program. The purpose in using such

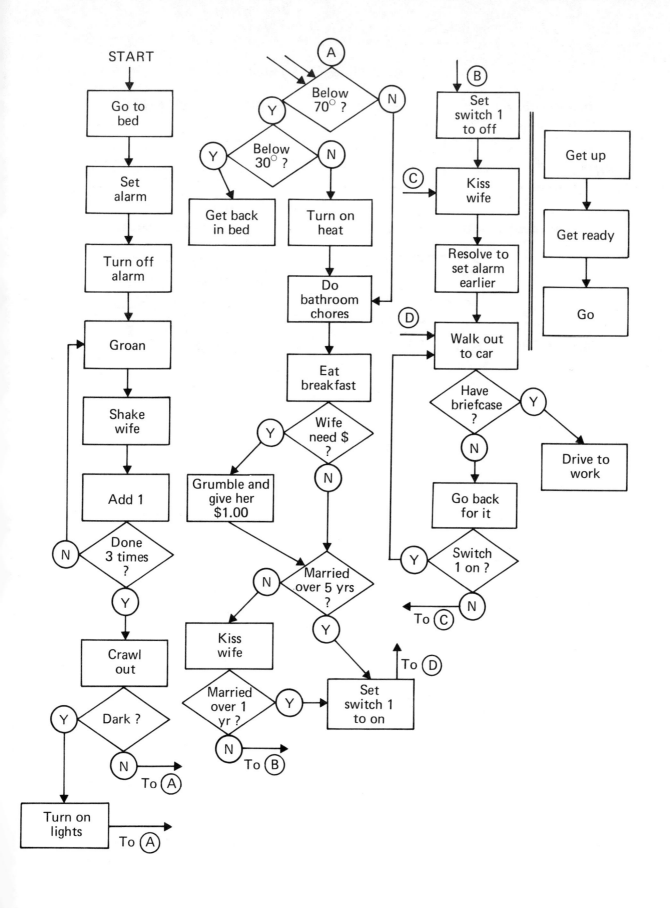

Basic Flowchart Symbols

Input/Output	Process	Flowline	Annotation

Specialized Input/Output Symbols

Punched Card

Magnetic Tape

Punched Tape

Document

Manual Input

Display

Communication Link

Specialized Process Symbols

Online Storage

Offline Storage

Decision

Predefined Process

Auxiliary Operation

Manual Operation

Additional Symbols

Connector

Terminal

a simple problem here is merely to show how flowcharting (another one of those strange computerese verbs) is done.

First, we'd set up a Data Summary that would look like this:

Room Size: 9 x 12 Feet = 12 Square Yards

CARPET NUMBER	BASIC PRICE PER SQ. YD.	DISCOUNT	SALES TAX	DELIVERY CHARGE	LIFE EXPECTANCY
1	$12.88	25%	6%	$15.00	10 YRS.
2	$13.10	NONE	NONE	NONE	10 YRS.
3	$15.00	1/3	6%	$15.00	10 YRS.
4	$20.00	NONE	6%	$15.00	10 YRS.

Then we would construct the flowchart, which could take several configurations; all of them, however, would look more or less like this:

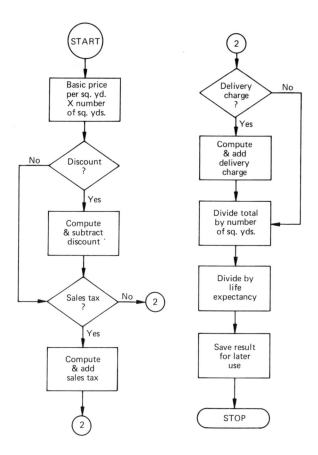

After the above computations have been completed for each carpet, the computer would examine the results to determine which deal offers the best value (i.e. lowest price per square yard per year).

The end result would be a "decision" by the computer as to which carpet represents the best value. (Inasmuch as the problem is hypothetical rather than actual, I have not taken the time or trouble to work out the solution. Compulsive readers are, of course, free to do that themselves.)

How this flowchart would then be written as a program depends on the dictates of the specific computer on which the program is to run. The manual that comes with your computer will not only show you how to write a program for that particular machine, but will give you examples of what programs look like. The program below, written in BASIC, is for the Altair microcomputer and is used to set up a peripheral printer to function like a typewriter. (The program is reprinted courtesy of Pertec Computer Corp., Microsystems Division.)

```
10 CLEAR2000
20 INPUT "DO YOU WANT TO CREATE
   A NEW LETTER";A$
30 IFLEFT$(A$,1)="Y"THENA$="O"
   ELSEA$="I"
40 LINEINPUT"ENTER THE NAME OF
   THE LETTER?";B$
50 A=INSTR(B$,","):IFA=OTHENDN
   =O:GOTO70
60 DN=VAL(MID$(B$,A+1,1)):B$=
   LEFT$(BS,A-1)
70 OPENA$,1,B$,DN
80 IFA$="I"THEN120
90 LINEINPUTC$:IFLEFT$(C$,4)=
   "END!"ORLEFT$(C$,4)="end!"
   THEN170
100 IFLEFT$(C$,4)="@PAG"ORLEFT$
   (C$,4)="@pag"THEN INPUT
   "PLEASE CHANGE PAGES AND HIT
   RETURN WHEN READY";A$
110 LPRINTC$:PRINT≭1,C$:GOTO90
```

```
120 INPUT"HIT RETURN WHEN PAPER
    IS READY";A$
130 LINEINPUT#1,C$
140 IFLEFT$(C$,4)="@PAG"ORLEFT$
    (C$,4)="@pag"THENPRINT
    "CHANGE PAGES!":GOTO120
150 LPRINTC$:IFEOF(1)THEN170
160 GOTO130
170 CLOSE1:END
```

• Software

The word "software" has been bandied about quite a bit among computerniks. One author, in a textbook for would-be programmers, states unequivocally:

> The software . . . consists of a collection of programs that make the computer easier to use and more effective. This collection of programs, supplied by the manufacturer for extending the capability of the equipment, should be clearly distinguished from *application programs* written by the *user* of the equipment to get his computational tasks performed. Sometimes the term software is mistakenly used for all aspects of programming.

These days, especially as far as microcomputers are concerned, the ways in which "software" is used effectively negates that last sentence. For our purposes, we may as well go along with the trend and regard all programming as software. (Nonapplication programs are usually known as "system software.")

One of the problems that has confronted the personal computing field for some time has been the unavailability of usable software. The computer operator, therefore, has had to devise his own programs or rely on those developed by hobbyists and published in the various periodicals catering to hobbyists (see Bibliography). That is all changing rapidly. One company (Scientific Research Inc.) has announced the publication of a BASIC Software Library, consisting of five volumes, ranging in price from $9.95 for the "experi-menter's programs" to $39.95 for the "advanced business" volume. The five books cover a wide range, including billing, inventory, payroll, bookkeeping, games, applications in mathematics, in engineering, in statistics, etc. The programs are supposedly written in "compatible BASIC immediately executable in ANY computer with at least 4K . . ." This is not to promote or endorse Scientific Research's Software Library; the foregoing intelligence is derived from their advertisement in a magazine. But it is a good example of how the scarcity of software for microcomputers is rapidly becoming past history.

Manufacturers of microcomputers also have software available for use on their machines. For example, the Radio Shack's TRS-80 system, a microcomputer virtually ready to plug in and operate, comes equipped with a game package. Also available, at nominal costs, are a payroll program for twelve employees, a math education program, a kitchen program which includes menus, conversion tables, and a message center, and a personal finance program. All of these programs are on tape cassettes. (Again, this is not a promotion or an endorsement of the TRS-80 system or the available software.)

• The Bootstrap Loader

In view of the fact that the computer is promoted as a tool of humankind, designed and intended to save hours—indeed, days and months—of work, why shouldn't a computer be able to take care of itself? As a matter of fact, it often can. Very large computer installations have all kinds of safety and fail-safe operations built in, covering everything from fire, breaking and entering, and theft of data, to simple loss of power either because of a blackout or because some dummy inadvertently flipped the wrong switch. The damage that can be done to hardware in a large computer system by simply turning off the current would be monumental were it not for fail-safe contingencies within the system itself. The loss of software and data that can result from power cutoff is significant to both large and small computer systems.

But what we are talking about here is programming. One of the finer touches in computing is the *bootstrap loader,* deriving, as one might suspect, from the long-standing and laudable American tradition of lifting oneself by one's own bootstraps. A bootstrap loader—or, as it is more often called, simply bootstrap—is a program that contains only a few instructions. Its purpose is to tell the computer that a quantity of data and a set of instructions are located in an I/O device. The bootstrap program then proceeds to load that data and/or information into the computer. In effect, then, the bootstrap is a program for loading in another program. Generally, bootstrap loaders are preprogrammed into read-only memory (ROM); however, if you see a microcomputer with a front panel consisting of a number of switches and LEDs (light-emitting diode read-outs), chances are that the operator enjoys switching in the bootstrap loader himself. Once that is done, however, the bootstrap takes over and loads the remainder of the program into the computer.

● Programmable Calculators

No discussion of programming would be complete without mentioning programmable calculators. A programmable calculator is something less than a computer but certainly something more than an adding machine. Perhaps the primary difference between a programmable calculator and a full-fledged computer is that the calculator, after all, has somewhat limited capabilities. But technological advances, coupled with decreasing manufacturing costs, make the programmable calculator worth considering as an alternative

to the microcomputer, especially for certain business applications. As the executive of one calculator manufacturer commented: "Users of programmable calculators have at their fingertips the equivalent computational capability of a computer that cost about $70,000 in the late 1950s."

Programmable calculators should be considered in situations that involve the performance of repeated operations that are basically the same and where only the data varies. For example, these calculators could be quite useful in working out sales commissions, or converting various specifications to and from the metric system, or calculating compound interest. Most standard calculators are not capable of handling such problems easily, while a computer may be more than is needed.

There are two types of programmable calculators. The preprogrammed calculator has a number of functions that are "hard-wired" into the unit. The program is built into the device. For example, if a company prepares blueprints for submission to a government agency on a regular basis and those blueprints carry specifications given in standard measurements, a preprogrammed calculator could easily convert all of those specifications into the metric system.

Other programmable calculators are capable of accepting specially written programs. Such programs are available in several ways. Not surprisingly, a number of calculator manufacturers offer application software. Where software is not available, the user can, with some models, keep records of the "program" as he keys it into the calculator. On a number of models, however, one need only insert a card or a cartridge into the machine to have the program recorded for repeated use.

Many models of programmable calculators are compatible with a variety of peripherals, such as printers, usually available from the manufacturer. One major manufacturer is already marketing ROM chips carrying a vari-

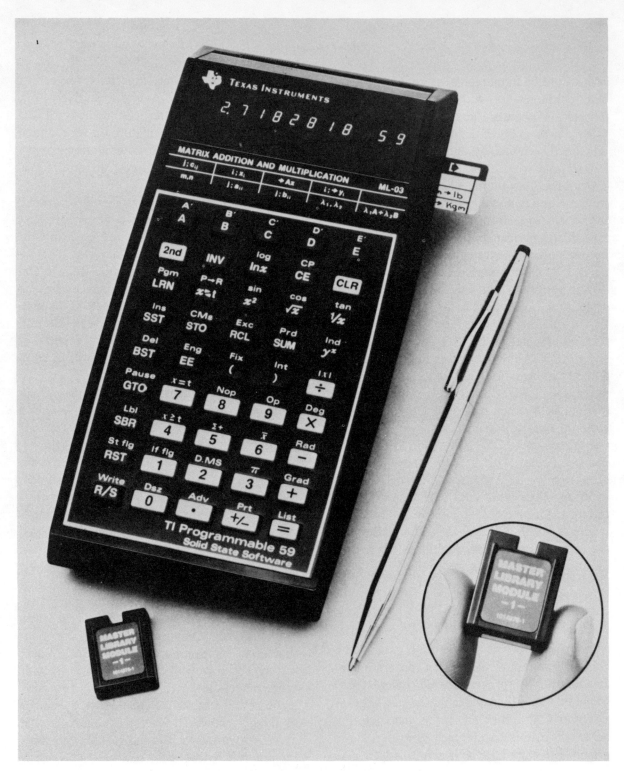

A programmable calculator. The card that has been inserted near the top of the calculator is for a "program" written by the user. The tiny cartridges contain softwear available for the unit. Courtesy Texas Instruments

ety of application programs that need only be plugged into the calculator.

Programmable calculators are available in a broad range of sizes, from those that slip easily into a pocket to those that occupy about the same desk space as a small typewriter. Prices start at well under $100.

Clearly, the microcomputer is no longer merely a hobbyist's diversion with which to play games and indulge in technological mysteries, the solutions to which are shared among a somewhat arcane group.

Microcomputers are ready to go to work.

8

PUTTING YOUR COMPUTER TO WORK

Setting aside for the moment such practical—but admittedly limited—uses of microprocessors in such things as hand-held calculators and household appliances, it must be acknowledged that the real impetus to personal computing came from the computer hobbyist. Now, the dictionary defines a hobby as an "occupation, activity, or interest . . . engaged in primarily for pleasure; a pastime." It was no surprise, therefore, that most hobbyists, when confronted by nonenthusiasts with the question, "But what practical use does your home computer have?," responded with a shrug, a sigh, and barely concealed chagrin. Usually, the stammered reply had something to do with the possibilities, potentials, and, almost guiltily, fun and games. In an article written in 1976 for *Science Digest,* I said:

> Claude Kagan, a Western Electric researcher, once suggested to a reporter that by putting physical details—height, weight, age, etc.—of all the people you know into a computer, the computer could then tell whether a stranger was ringing your front doorbell. (Presumably, you could at that point seal up the peephole, which would provide the same information.) Other hobbyists talk of programming home computers to catalog a record collection and balance checkbooks. Also suggested, but apparently never actually tried, is programming a home computer to vacuum the living room or mow the lawn.

That same year, in an article for *Cavalier,* I wrote:

> Almost since the appearance of the first computers, the people involved with them have gotten the machines to play chess and tic-tac-toe, or draw amusing pictures or engage in sophisticated word games. Now, with the advent of the MPU, computer lovers can play these games in their own basements. Still, computer hobbyists are no worse than other hobbyists who love gadgetry for its own sake; not everyone who owns a fancy camera takes good pictures.

Since those articles were written, however, several developments have changed—and are changing—both the attitude toward and the uses of microcomputers, rapidly removing the little marvels from the realm of the fun-loving hobbyist to the domain of the practical householder and/or businessperson.

Price. At a period in our economic history that will live in infamy for its apparently never-ending upward spiral of prices, the electronics industry generally and the microcomputer industry specifically stand out as reversals of this trend. Virtually everything involved in microcomputers, from prepackaged software to the most sophisticated equipment, continues to decline in price. In my *Science Digest* article, I mentioned microcomputer kits retailing for about a thousand dollars on up, which, while not exactly cheap, was certainly far below anybody's conception of what a computer ought to cost. Yet, only eighteen months later, a complete microcomputer, already built and ready to plug in, could be purchased for only six or seven hundred dollars. Technology and production are the underlying reasons for microcomputer prices either holding the line or actually declining. As refinements in the manufacturing processes, as well as in the items being manufactured, continue to increase, the costs of producing them continue to decrease. Furthermore, as more and more people become interested in microcomputers, more and more are sold, and in all but the worst-managed business operations, increased sales invariably lead at least to the potential for lower prices.

Kits and parts. When microcomputers first appeared on the scene, putting them together required the hands of a surgeon and the dedication of a martyr, along with considerable knowledge of and experience with computers and electronics. But increased technology has brought not only lower prices but relative ease of construction and operation. Furthermore, those little pieces of board bristling with wires and pins that are characteristic of microprocessors are now capable of performing many more tasks and functions than their early predecessors.

Complete systems. Perhaps the most significant development in the popularization of home computers is the availability of complete systems, not only from computer stores and electronics dealers but from other retailers such as department stores and large mail-order catalog houses. (A number of major retailers have announced plans to begin carrying such products, and if your favorite department store does not have them yet, no doubt it will soon.) The main advantages of these complete systems are that they are compact, they require virtually no prior knowledge of electronics or computers, and they require practically no assembly. Obviously, their appearance on the market offers the use of a sophisticated and versatile computer to millions of people who otherwise would not have such access. While these machines are not cheap, they are priced well within the reach of a vast segment of the American population. I have seen, in prefectly ordinary homes, electric typewriters, TV sets, pianos, hi-fi stereo equipment, refrigerators, and many other amenities of contemporary life, each of which costs far more than most of these microcomputers. (We shall have more to say about the virtues and evils of computer kits *vis-à-vis* factory-built systems in Chapter 10.)

Language. The development of high-level computer languages—most significantly, BASIC—makes it possible for the average citizen to communicate with a computer in a language that they can both understand. The appearance and growth of microcomputer magazines, originally intended for the hobbyist, are rapidly expanding the language capabilities not only of computers, but also of the people who own them.

Software. From the very beginning of microprocessing as a hobby, software—or, more accurately, its absence—presented a serious problem. Typically, such software as did exist involved game-playing, and hobbyists who developed their own programs began exchanging them with other hobbyists, either through computer clubs or through the magazines. This practice continues, and as the number of users increases and the degree of sophistication among users increases, no doubt the sharing of software will become a significant aspect of personal computing, as, indeed, it should. But manufacturers of microcomputers soon realized that if they were to expand the market for their equipment, they would also have to expand the capability of a greater number of consumers to use that equipment. The result is that a considerable amount of software is now being made available by the companies who make the computers. This is not particularly innovative; the corporate giants who manufacture huge computers have always supplied software to their customers. So have companies set up specifically for the purpose of developing and marketing software. These practices have now filtered down to the microcomputer industry so that manufacturers, software companies, and users are all making software available to the microcomputer user.

As a direct result of these newer, smarter, and easier-to-operate computers, much of life's tedium can be relegated to a machine. To be sure, there are limitations to the type and especially to the size of a task that a microcomputer can be expected to perform. A computer has only so much memory and there is a limit as to how much memory can be added on even if that limit ultimately is determined by financial rather than technological considerations. Furthermore, a microcomputer can do many of the things that a large computer can, but certainly not all of them—at least, not nearly as fast. If you operate a business that employs fifty or sixty people, you can probably set up a payroll program that can be conveniently run on a microcomputer. But if you are responsible for the payroll for two or three thousand people, by the time your microcomputer finishes the run, most of your employees will be ready for retirement.

There are really two kinds of limitations on the various tasks a microcomputer can perform: (1) the limitations of the computer itself; and (2) the limitations of your own imagination and creativity in developing programs that use your microcomputer to its maximum capacity. The computer applications which follow, therefore, should be regarded merely as suggestions for possible use

and should not be regarded as restrictions on the versatility of microcomputers.

• Record-keeping

This is a general, broad, all-purpose category that is likely to mean all things to all people. For a physician, for example, record-keeping with a microcomputer means that he can maintain all of his patients' records in a safe, convenient, compact location—the computer system. For the phonograph-record collector, setting up a filing system by using the computer is a task of the utmost simplicity. The same is true for someone with a large personal library. One need only assign each new acquisition a number, in sequence. In other words, if the last book or record you acquired is numbered 142, then the next one you acquire will be numbered 143. Using those numbers as a basis, you can then input enough information to keep a handy, accurate file. Cross-referencing becomes a simple matter. The book collector can enter the data under author, title of book, subject matter of book, name of illustrator, and any other details that could prove useful, including—if the collector buys, sells, and trades rare volumes—the purchase price and date of purchase. The record collector, following the same general idea, could cross-reference each new entry by composer, performer, type of music, type of instrumental solo, and any other pertinent information. As for the physician, with a modicum of programming, he or she can easily cross-reference patients according to type of illness, sex, age, socioeconomic level, etc., so that at a moment's notice he or she could extract interesting, useful, and perhaps even vital information about the state of a community's health.

Microcomputer owners who belong to organizations could suddenly become very popular by offering to maintain any number of records for that organization. Membership rolls, financial records, and other types of files could be stored for ready retrieval by your microcomputer. In fact, the storage media dedicated to such record-keeping might even provide a tax deduction if the organization is charitable or not-for-profit. (It is always advisable to consult an accountant about such things; I will not accompany you to the IRS office.)

Perhaps the most useful application of microcomputers for purposes of record-keeping is that of personal finances. I predict that in the near future, perhaps even by the time this book appears in print, you will be able to buy software that will enable you to maintain clear and accurate financial records at home. But even if that prediction should fail to materialize, it is still possible, with relative ease, to involve a microcomputer in financial planning for the family.

You could begin by inputting a rough budget: anticipated annual income, known expenses for the year (rent or mortgage, heating costs, approximate utility costs—based on the previous year's costs—insurance, tuition, etc.). You would then add the amount you are prepared to allow for so-called discretionary expenditures such as entertainment, vacation, etc. The program should include some predetermined rules for dealing with unexpected expenses. For example, if automobile maintenance or heating bills exceed a given monthly limit, then entertainment or vacation costs are to be reduced by whatever amount is decided upon.

When a bill comes in, the amount of the bill and the category to which it applies are keyed into the computer so that a comparison can be made between the planned expenses and the actual expenses. In this way, with the help of the computer, you could keep a continual watch on your budget, adjusting as necessary. (According to one report, there should now be on the market a program for bill-juggling.)

Another form of financial record-keeping is the relatively simple process of checking one's bank balance. If you find yourself writing out some twenty-five to thirty checks each month, even if you are proficient with numbers and own a good calculator, it probably takes you at least fifteen minutes to check out the balance in your checkbook against the monthly statement you receive from the bank. With a microcomputer, this could be handled as an ongoing process. Every few days, you would simply key in the amounts of the checks you have written. Your program would provide for flagging those checks that have not yet cleared the bank at the time the statement arrives. Once the program has been designed and is running, you could probably check your bank balance in a minute or two, if not in a matter of seconds.

It seems almost too obvious to mention that one of the best applications of a microcomputer for record-keeping is in the operation of a small business. A microprocessor is ideal for inventory control, payroll, accounts receivable, accounts payable, interest rates, mortgage rates, amortization, and a host of other records and data that are tedious and annoying when they have to be accumulated for any reason—usually for tax purposes—but which become much less so when the data, a bit at a time, is input to the computer and can be recalled literally with the touch of a button or two.

● **Investment Portfolios**

Many years ago, I served time as a mutual-fund salesman and learned a little about stocks and bonds (most of which, mercifully, has been forgotten). There were many "systems" for making market predictions, ranging from sunspot cycles to an intricate formula of economic trends and factors such as the prime interest rate, the price of gold, gross national product, etc. The one that stands out most in my mind was a system which claimed that the movement of the market would follow that of the hemlines of women's skirts by approximately six months; that is, if skirts rose, approximately six months later the market would rise. If they fell, the market would do likewise. This method was remarkable not so much for its attractiveness as a means of keeping track of the stock market but because it was surprisingly accurate. Unfortunately, recent fashion trends and sociological changes in attitudes toward conformity have made this technique inoperable. I maintain, however, that it is about as sensible and accurate an approach to market predictability as any other, including one which involves careful tracking and analysis of such things as the Dow-Jones average with a computer. At one time, particularly in the early days of computers, people who had access to computers spent a lot of time playing around with stock market predictions. For some reason, such activity seems to have diminished greatly—at least, it is no longer discussed very much. That may be because even a computer, however sophisticated, is incapable of dealing with the frivolities of the investment markets or because those who have failed have simply given up and stopped talking about it, while those who have succeeded prefer to keep their secret to themselves. If you are obsessed with the idea of computerizing a system for winning at stocks and bonds—or, for that matter, any other form of gambling, such as blackjack or horse racing—then, by all means, put your computer to good use. You may actually hit upon one of those well-kept secrets. Even if such secrets do not actually exist, you should not be deterred by the failure of others. After all, Thomas Edison and Albert Einstein persisted in areas where others failed. And patent attorneys are constantly turning away would-be clients who are convinced that they have invented the true perpetual-motion machine.

Perhaps a discussion of computerized stock market predictions properly belongs in the next chapter, "Fun and Games," but quite seriously, it is not a possibility that should be lightly tossed aside. After all, stock market behavior is at least somewhat cyclical and such cycles do seem to occur with some regularity. I remember, as a mutual-fund salesman, being taken on a tour of the offices of what was then a relatively new and very hot mutual fund, managed by a company headed by a young man who was then affectionately referred to as "the *wunderkind* of Wall Street." The young president's office had two walls covered, from ceiling to floor, with a chart showing the New York *Times* stock averages for a great many years (I cannot remember the exact time period covered). Only occasionally was there an erratic dip or unexpected high. It was easy to see, by looking at the chart, how the market moves not in volcanic eruptions or lead-weight descents, but rather in a fairly smooth-flowing, wavelike pattern of ups and downs. Certainly, it can do no harm to place so-called "mind bets" in certain specific investments (i.e. the stocks of a particular company, or the bonds of a particular municipality, or certain specific commodities), industries (aerospace, electronics, entertainment and leisure, etc.), or in trading areas (stock exchanges, commodity exchanges, over-the-counter). If you see some sort of trend emerging, one which continues over an extended period of time and appears to offer the possibilities of predictability, you could follow that trend to see whether you have, in fact, hit upon a winning system, at which point you could risk some hard cash. (I want it clearly understood, however, that none of the foregoing is to be construed as a recommendation or endorsement on my part. I have no idea whether the electronics or aerospace industries are worthy investments now or later. Proceed at your own risk.)

Of course, there is much more to the possibilities of a working relationship between investments and microcomputers. Certainly, a home computer offers one of the best ways to keep track of one's own investment portfolio, particularly when you remember that "investment portfolio" covers stocks, bonds, mutual-fund holdings, mortgages (the kind where someone pays you, not the other way around), United States Savings Bonds, savings accounts at savings banks and savings and loan associations, and life insurance policies, particularly those that pay dividends and/or annuities. If you are holding, for example, so-called "blue chip" or "gilt edge" stocks, happily collecting quarterly dividends, you may not realize that given the current rate of inflation, your money might earn more for you if you sold those stocks at the current market rate and reinvested the proceeds from that sale in something yielding a higher rate. If you are socking away funds in a savings account against some future goal, such as retirement or college tuition, you may be surprised to learn that the inflation rate, your tax bracket, and the rate of interest you receive for your savings all combine to gradually chip away at a sensible retirement or tuition fund. Perhaps that money would serve you better in municipal bonds, which, while paying a lower interest rate, are nontaxable and may, therefore, provide greater earnings for you. A microcomputer can be an extremely handy method of keeping track of the entire portfolio, the purchase price of each item in that portfolio, the interest or dividends each item yields, and the current market value of each investment. As simple a technique as dollar cost averaging can be made even more simple with the help of a home computer. (Dollar cost averaging, as the term suggests, involves averaging out the cost of a particular investment by investing a fixed amount of money in the same stock at regular intervals. Your money buys more shares when the market is low and fewer shares when the market is high, but the average *cost* per share is lower than the average *price* per share. Yes, I know, this is a book about computers and not about investments.)

Bearing in mind that a computer can perform calculations, make comparisons, and then make decisions based on those comparisons, a microcomputer would seem to be an eminently sensible method of keeping track of an investment.

• Mailing Lists

On any typical day, you are likely to receive a letter or statement from your bank, a catalog from a mail-order firm, an offer from a magazine inviting you to subscribe, and many other pieces of mail designed, in one way or another, to separate you from a portion of your money. In almost every case, that mail has been addressed by a computer. Commercial mailing lists are usually maintained by a computer in accordance with various categories. Geography, income level, size and type of home, political party affiliation, marital status, number and/or ages of children, occupation or profession—all these and others are logical types of mailing lists for various businesses to maintain. In fact, the reason you often receive several copies of the same piece of mail is that you are on more than one mailing list. (In our house, one of the more pleasant diversions that the daily mail brings is seeing how many different ways the name "Grosswirth" can be spelled.) The application of similar techniques can be most helpful in maintaining a personal mailing list and is easy to arrange with a microcomputer.

It is perhaps a little silly and pretentious to go to a computer to find out Aunt Harriet's address when you want to send her a birthday card, when all you have to do is flip to the proper section of the address book that you keep near the telephone. But suppose the month of December is drawing near and you find that, as usual, you will be sending greeting cards to perhaps a hundred or more people. Some of those people will be receiving Christmas cards while others will probably expect Hannukah cards. Going through that address book a name at a time to determine who gets what kind of card can make a serious dent in the holiday spirit, whereas punching a couple of buttons on your microcomputer can separate the Jews from the Christians in no time, for once a not-unworthy process.

Now that you have the list separated, you and your spouse will certainly go over it, a name at a time, to determine whether "they" sent "us" a card last year. By keying in the names of people you want to send cards to and those you have received cards from, at the appropriate time you could have your microcomputer print out address labels for those people from whom you received cards last year, labels for the people to whom you will send cards regardless of whether they sent any last year, and a list of the people about whom a decision has to be made. There are those who will argue that computerizing a holiday-card mailing list and printing out the names and addresses make the process of sending such cards cold, impersonal, and commercial-looking. My reply to such arguments is that the mailing of holiday cards *en masse* with the name of the sender already imprinted on the inside of the card is already cold, impersonal, and commercial—to such an extent that making life a little simpler by using a personal computer will do little, if anything, to make matters worse.

I am at a loss to understand why what little literature there is in the personal computer field has failed to point out the value of a microcomputer for maintaining a mailing list beyond the Christmas card application. It seems to me to be an eminently useful occupation to separate one's personal mailing list into certain categories: husband's relatives, wife's relatives, husband's friends, wife's friends, mutual friends, children's friends, business associates, etc. Surely everyone has had or will have a situation in which one or more of these categories must be separated from the entire mailing list. Invitations to a party or a wedding,

people who have to be called in case of an emergency or a death in the family, people to whom social announcements must be sent—how much easier to key all of this data into storage once and have it available for almost instant use whenever it is needed.

• A Computerized Kitchen

It has actually been suggested that the owner of a microcomputer take a complete inventory of the family larder, key the quantities into the computer and every time an item is used, key that in, too, so that the computer can alert the dedicated and efficient homemaker when supplies are running low. In my opinion, utilizing the computer for such purposes is sheer nonsense. Just imagine telling your computer that you have a dozen frankfurters in the refrigerator and then, three days later, when you want a quick lunch, running over to the machine to let it know that you are about to consume two of those frankfurters and a can of baked beans. In my house, such a system would break down in a matter of days, if not hours. There are, however, some very practical and time-saving applications of the microcomputer to the kitchen, not the least of which is, in fact, an inventory—not an inventory of the contents of the refrigerator or the cupboard over the sink, but an inventory of long-term supplies.

Many families have long ago recognized the value of owning a deep freeze which sits in the basement and accommodates large quantities of meat and other frozen foods, purchased in quantity when prices are low and used as needed. Certainly, an inventory of such supplies can be kept by a microcomputer. An inventory of this type serves two purposes: first, of course, it lets you know when you are running low on some item. Second, it lets you know, should there be a particularly good value available, whether you have room for the product you want to purchase. Obviously, this method need not apply only to frozen food. If you have the storage space for canned goods, laundry products, paper goods, and other nonperishables, it makes sense to buy in quantity when such items are on sale. In many communities, there are wholesale markets which sell at close-to-wholesale prices to consumers willing to buy in case lots and cart the stuff home in their own cars.

Another useful application of the microcomputer to the kitchen is in the filing of recipes. Dedicated cooks often have efficient and elaborate (although the two terms are not necessarily synonymous) recipe files consisting of file-card boxes, scrapbooks, notebooks, and albums, filled with recipes clipped from newspapers and magazines, and a quantity of recipes stored inside the chef's brain, destined to die when the cook does. One of the very first practical applications of a microcomputer is the computerization of all of those recipes. Consider, for a moment, just a few of the possibilities. Based upon how the data is entered, a microcomputer could yield up in a trice all the available recipes for chocolate desserts. In the event of a less-than-abundantly stocked pantry, an occurrence that usually coincides with the arrival of unexpected guests, a mere touch at the computer terminal can deliver all of the recipes available that include one common ingredient—say, tuna fish. The home computer can be used to plan menus. "I have a chicken," the cook says to the computer. "What goes well with chicken?" The computer answers immediately, in accordance with the cook's tastes. Thus, if the user believes that succotash and spinach go well with chicken, the computer will remind him or her that this is a preferred combination (although not one that is preferred by me). Spend a couple of hours with your input terminal in one hand and a good calorie chart in the other, and forever after the computer can give you the total calorie count of a planned meal. For people on special diets, the computer can store the nutritive composition of foods so that you know immediately what to feed Uncle Herman, who is coming to dinner tonight and is on a low-sodium regimen.

The other night, I decided to take a brief respite from the creative effort which is this book and try out a new and relatively simple recipe for cookies. The recipe calls for three eggs. To my dismay, I discovered that there was only one egg in the refrigerator. Attempting to divide the remainder of the ingredients by one third was more trouble than I was willing to invest in the project, so I turned instead to the self-hypnosis of television. Had I but properly programmed a microcomputer, it could easily have told me what one third of all of the other ingredients in that cookie recipe would be.

The uses of a microcomputer for someone who spends a great deal of time in the kitchen seem almost infinite. Conversion of weights and measures, decreasing or expanding recipes, menu planning, calorie counting, keeping track of cooking times, keeping track of people's favorite foods or food restrictions, making price comparisons, are some of the applications I can think of. No doubt, you can think of a great many more.

• A Computerized Environment

If you have a thermostat, it will turn on the furnace (or the air conditioner) when the temperature of the area in which the thermostat is located differs from the one set on the thermostat. It will do that regardless of whether the room is occupied, about to be occupied, or just recently vacated. But if a computer is programmed with the general habits of the members of the household and if it is equipped with the necessary sensors, it could turn heating and cooling devices on and off in a pattern that is compatible with the goings and comings of the family. It could also perform such functions as turning on washing ma-

65

chines or dishwashers at those times of day when the electricity rate is lower. One rather sophisticated application is the controlling of a lawn sprinkler. Sensors placed in the soil could measure the amount of moisture and feed that data to the computer, which would then determine if more moisture is required. If so, it turns on the sprinkler. Other sensors measure the amount of sunlight to make sure that the sprinkling is not done at a time when the sun is in a position to damage the foliage.

An extremely valuable application of a microcomputer would be that of giving a home a lived-in look when the occupants are away. The computer could be programmed to turn lights on and off at random and cause the radio or TV set to play during hours when people would normally be home.

By now, you have probably realized that almost all of the applications mentioned in environmental control can be accomplished without a computer; thermostats, timers, photoelectric cells, and moderately priced security devices can be purchased to achieve these very same effects. Certainly, that makes sense and it would be extravagant to purchase a microcomputer just for these purposes. Furthermore, to program a computer to perform such tasks requires a considerable amount of knowledge and experience as well as the expense of the admittedly unique "peripherals" that would be required to achieve these ends. Again, no argument. The point to remember, however, is that a microcomputer is a multipurpose device. It would probably be pointless to buy one for the control of one's home environment, but if you are going to buy one anyway for other reasons, it would be just as extravagant to avoid at least a consideration of this kind of application for the machine.

In the foreseeable future, it is very likely that all new homes will come equipped with some kind of microcomputer, a kind of centralized "brain" controlling and responding to the "nerves" extending throughout the house.

Such a system is not beyond the realm of possibility right now. It is expensive and difficult to install, so that while it exists, it is limited in use and affordable only by the very wealthy. But as we have seen, rapidly advancing technology continues to diminish costs and in a very few years, the average homeowner will be able to afford his own computer and among the things that the computer will do is control the home's environment.

Such predictions tend to conjure up images of the science fiction movie in which an obedient and tireless robot serves breakfast in bed, washes the dishes, and sees the children safely off to school. As far-fetched and remote as such images seem to be, they are not beyond the realm of possibility or practicality. After all, millions of Americans are awakened to the sound of gentle music. If they fail to respond, the sound gets louder and gradually harsher, changing from music to a chime to a loud buzzer. At the same time, their coffee automatically starts perking, their bath water starts heating up in the boiler in the basement, and warm air is flowing through the heat registers in the bedroom. Had you suggested that any of this was possible at the beginning of this century, you would have been laughed out of town.

• Programmed Learning

Programmed learning is a method of teaching which involves a carefully structured presentation of the information to be learned. In this method, the learning process begins with the simplest and most readily understood information and gradually increases in difficulty and complexity. Along the way, there are stages, built into the program, at which the learner tests himself.

There are a number of advantages to programmed learning. First, it permits the learner to proceed at his own pace. Second, it enables him to absorb the information one step at a time. Third, it permits him to determine, as he proceeds, whether he is, in fact, learning. If he is not, there are usually drills and techniques built into the program for reinforcing the learning process.

Lots of programmed learning materials exist in book form, but there are also devices known as "teaching machines." These can be highly sophisticated and very elegant electronic setups, but almost everyone has seen a much simpler version, usually available in most toy departments. In this version, the teaching machine consists of a box with a series of little windows or slides. A problem— say, a multiplication problem—is presented. The user offers the solution to the problem and can then see, by exposing another window, whether he has gotten the right answer. In some versions of this machine, the user cannot proceed to the next question until he corrects his answer to the current question.

Of all of the tasks for which a microcomputer is suited, probably none can be handled more effectively than programmed learning. The presence of children of school or preschool age in a household should be a strong inducement for owning a home computer. Already, programmed-learning software exists. One manufacturer of a complete, ready-to-plug-in computer system offers software for learning math at a very low price. Additional software from a variety of sources is available. More is certainly on the way.

What is perhaps more interesting, however, is the fact that anyone who owns a microcomputer and knows how to program it can purchase programmed learning materials in book form and, using fairly simple programming skills, write a computer program and turn his microcomputer into a highly efficient teaching machine.

(If any of the foregoing is a little confusing, reread it, keeping in mind that the word "programmed" is, perforce, being used in two different ways. In one instance, it refers to the programming that is done for your computer. In other instances, it is used to describe a particular form of learning material which may or may not be computerized; computerization has nothing to do with "programmed learning," as that phrase is defined. Is that clear now?)

• Word Processing

Word processing as a computerized concept has its origins in the giant corporations, but its appeal to those involved in personal computers is undeniable. Essentially, word processing involves the following basic concepts:

First, you compose whatever it is you are going to compose—a letter, a manuscript, advertising copy, a sales, technical, or instruction manual, etc.—on an input device that displays. That can be a typewriter, a CRT (cathode ray tube terminal, the video-screen type of I/O device), or a Teletypewriter. You can then edit, making corrections, deletions, changes, and additions on the same input device. Everything goes into the computer and, when you are finished and press the right button, the computer prints out a perfect copy, free of errors, and set up in any way you specify. It can be single-spaced, double-spaced, justified right and left, with alternate paragraphs indented—just about any kind of layout you can imagine.

Since you have reached this far in this book, you probably don't need this admonition, but I will include it, anyway: the computer does not make typing mistakes. But neither can it correct bad spelling, faulty grammar, or improper punctuation that is fed to it by the operator. (Unless, of course, it has been preprogrammed to correct such errors, a nicety not yet available for most microcomputers. Indeed, many large computers are ill-equipped to handle some of these problems. Most major newspapers are prepared by word-processing systems, a fact easily detectable by the annoying and often ludicrous way in which words are sometimes hyphenated at the end of a line.)

In its simplest form, a word-processing system makes the additions, deletions, or changes just mentioned. Ideally, however, a good word-processing system should also be able to move sections of copy around. There are word-processing routines that can seek out every occurrence of a single word or phrase in the text, remove it, and insert another word or phrase. It is possible to have this desirable feature in a microcomputer system, provided there is enough memory.

It has been suggested that one practical use of a word-processing system is the production of those abominable Christmas letters that some people delight in sending. By breaking down the information that would go into such a letter, it would then be possible to select those pieces of information that a given recipient or group of recipients would be most interested in receiving. Then, while reviewing the mailing list, one could single out either the specific topics or the individual paragraphs that would be most likely to intrigue the individual on the list. The computer, having no sense of taste or decency, would then type the letter as instructed. The computerized letter could even be "personalized" by inserting the recipient's name at various places in the letter.

A far more worthwhile use of a word-processing routine is a variation on that theme. A system could be easily be set up for a charitable organization, a religious group, or a school, selecting information or paragraphs that might be of specific interest to the recipient. For example, a school with classes ranging from kindergarten through eighth grade could send out letters in which the opening paragraphs would make reference to the grade level relevant to the recipient's child. A religious congregation could similarly feature, in the opening paragraphs, the timing and convenience of religious services, religious school facilities for children and adults, activities for single people, young people, married people, old people, etc.

For a sensible word-processing system, you will probably need a microcomputer with at least 16K of memory. That, however, is minimal; 32K should be considered for a more complete system.

Also needed is some kind of mass data storage. For the most part, word-processing routines are sequential, and are therefore highly adaptable to tape cassettes for storage. But if speed is important, floppy-disk storage is advised.

If you decide to use your microcomputer for word processing, investigate the possibilities and availability of a word-processing program written in machine language. You will remember that a microcomputer must "translate" the high-level language to machine language and that this requires more memory than if the program were written in machine language directly. Now you are adding a program for word processing, taking up still more memory. In other words, first the program that changes the high-level language into machine language must be loaded into the computer. Then the word-processing program itself must be loaded. Finally, the copy that is to be processed is input. The need for memory with a substantial capacity becomes obvious. If, however, you can use a word-processing program that is written in machine language, you are, in effect, freeing up a good portion of the memory for use by the text to be edited.

The ultimate goal of a word-processing system is typewritten, error-free copy. Various typewriter terminals are available, and some of them are probably compatible with the microcomputer you own or are thinking of buying. One of the more popular types is the IBM Selectric and other terminals based on the type-ball used in Selectrics. Remember, however, that while most microcomputers use the ASCII code, the IBM Selectric and machines based on the IBM Selectric ball use a different kind of code, so it is important, before investing in any of these terminals, to make certain that there is some means, through code conversion, of interfacing the terminal with your microcomputer.

Another drawback to word-processing systems is the cost. At the time this book was written, I was told that a microcomputer, complete with the necessary peripherals for an efficient word-processing system, would cost in the neighborhood of three to four thousand dollars. Which is why this book has been written by a somewhat more old-fashioned, but less expensive, method of word processing.

• Business Applications

So far, in discussing the various ways of putting a microcomputer to work, we have, for the most part, confined ourselves to uses within a home setting. In doing so, we have, willy-nilly, crisscrossed the line between personal use and business use. But when it comes to business applications that require such data as detailed daily inventories, up-to-date accounts receivable, expenses, posting to various bookkeeping accounts, sales and production data, etc., we are beginning to move away somewhat from the relatively low cost of microcomputers.

For one thing, it is recommended that a microcomputer for use in a small business should have a minimum of 24K memory; the more memory, the costlier the system. It is also recommended that disks be used for memory and storage; disks cost more than tape cassettes. In most instances, a video-type terminal will probably be needed for keeping track of input and output, but some method of obtaining *hard copy* (printed sheets) will also be necessary. In addition, mass storage should be provided for by means of a tape cassette peripheral. This is necessary because data that is entered on disks and subsequently removed

each day can be "filed" in the tape cassette as a data file backup. (Of course, "floppies" can also be used for backup files.)

Another important consideration in using a microcomputer for general business applications is the effect on the business that a possible breakdown might have. Computers, alas, do occasionally break down. That could mean anywhere from several hours to several days without the use of the computer, depending upon one's own ability to make repairs and the availability of parts and service. An important consideration, therefore, before using a microcomputer to run a small business, is whether that business can function when the computer does not. Before entrusting your business to a computer, make sure that the following conditions exist:

1. The computer itself is a well-constructed model that has been tested through use and comes from a known, reliable manufacturer.

2. Application programs for the computer are readily available. It may be necessary to revise existing application programs somewhat; this can often be done with a minimum of difficulty.

3. The computer has a sufficient amount of memory to retain not only anticipated requirements, but a bit more in the event of unanticipated needs.

4. The computer has sufficient versatility to expand its capacity, both for memory and for peripherals.

5. It has a reliable disk-operating system.

6. Software, with sufficient flexibility to adapt to changing business conditions, is available.

7. A printer that will provide print-outs of programs and reports is, or can be, included in the system.

8. There is an adequate data backup provision, a means of storing programs and data for possible future use.

9. Adequate servicing of the equipment is available.

Upon reviewing the above checklist, it becomes apparent that microcomputers for business use are somewhat more complex and expensive than they are for home use. They are not, however, beyond the means of many small businesses. And they are, of course, a legitimate business expense. If you own and operate a small business, and the details and paperwork are beginning to get you down, you might want to have a long and serious discussion with your accountant about having a computer of your very own.

Once you do have one, it can help you escape from the pressures and trials of the everyday world. Those little electronic devils just love to play games with people.

9

FUN AND GAMES

Almost from the time the first practical computer began operating, people played games with it. Programmers, easily bored with such prosaic matters as actuarial tables, meteorological data, and atomic energy formulas, amused themselves by playing chess, checkers, and tic-tac-toe with computers. Kent Porter, in his excellent and highly recommended book *Computers Made Really Simple* (New York: Thomas Y. Crowell Company, 1976), wrote:

> In 1952, a man was heard on the radio describing the capabilities of the machine he supervised, and one of his comments was that it was unbeatable at tic-tac-toe. My own father had a comment that seems to summarize the overall feeling of America at that point in the computer's infancy: "It seems pretty silly to me to spend millions of dollars to build a machine to play tic-tac-toe."

Obviously—and understandably—the senior Mr. Porter had no way of foretelling, any more than the rest of us did, that this machine that played tic-tac-toe would change the shape of the world.

Nevertheless, the underlying philosophy of that comment is as true today for the would-be purchaser of a microcomputer as it was in the 1950s. Even the most rudimentary microcomputer is expensive by comparison to a chess set, a deck of cards, electronic video games, and a lot of other objects that can be used for amusement. Does the price justify the game-playing end? The answer is that it does if you think it does. This is, after all, a moral argument and one that can be applied to a trip to Las Vegas, an expensive hi-fi system, a limousine, an original work of art, or anything else for which there exists a cheaper, functional substitute that will readily fulfill the need. Obviously, then, need is not the issue. If your interests in a microcomputer rest solely in the areas of amusement, then whether to indulge yourself becomes a question to be debated between you, your finances, and whoever else in the world you may feel obliged to answer to. Just leave me out of it.

But the computer as game player suggests a much more subtle, perhaps even a philosophical, question. One writer has described the computer as an idiot. It cannot think. It cannot act on its own. It has no emotions, no feelings, no sense of right or wrong. No matter what the science fiction writers and filmmakers say, a computer has no will of its own; it is only a tool of humankind. If that is true, isn't asking a computer to play a game something like asking a camera to take a good picture? A camera will photograph whatever it is told to photograph. If it is a fancy camera, it will adjust itself to the lighting conditions and make a proper exposure. But it will photograph the ugly and the beautiful with complete equanimity. It will take a well-composed picture as well as a badly composed one. It will photograph the most inspiring religious image or the filthiest pornography. The esthetic quality of a photograph depends not on the camera but on the photographer. Similarly, how can a computer play a better game of chess or tic-tac-toe than a person can? We have already seen the answer: the machine operates logically, it makes comparisons among pieces of data, then makes decisions on the basis of those comparisons, and does it all at speeds that are inconceivable to most human minds. But isn't that the same as thinking? When a person makes a decision, doesn't that involve a process of taking different bits of data, weighing and comparing them, and making the necessary decision accordingly? Well, yes and no. At least one of the differences between a computer and a person is that the computer can never have certain types of data that the human mind contains. If a computer lets you win, it is not because the computer likes you or feels pity for you, but because it has been programmed to let you win. If a computer beats you every time, it is not because the machine hates you, but because it has more data, logic, and speed than you have. I once played tic-tac-toe with a microcomputer. At the outset, the machine offered me a range of difficulty, on a scale of 0 to 9, from which to choose. When I chose the low end of the difficulty scale, I won just about every game. When I chose the high end of the difficulty scale, I lost every time. No emotion was involved, at least not on the computer's part. Even when the CRT on which the games were displayed printed out, YOU LOSE AGAIN, DUMMY, the machine was only doing what it was programmed to do, a realization which

kept me from putting my fist through its immobile face.

Computer games, then, offer at least three benefits: (1) they amuse; (2) they can be educational; and (3) they can demonstrate very effectively to the average layman, who has neither interest in nor knowledge of computers, just how frail and faulty a thing the human brain is.

• Electronic Diversions

In a sense, the very act of building a microcomputer and expanding upon it is a kind of game. After all, home computing began as a hobby and still gets much of its impetus from hobbyists. We shall have more to say about constructing computers in the next chapter, but it is worth mentioning here that many thousands of people derive considerable pleasure from buying kits and putting them together. Such kits are available not only for MPUs but for peripherals, interfaces, and many of the other appurtenances involved in microcomputers. Advanced electronic hobbyists have even been known to buy some basic parts and put them together. If you hang around a computer store long enough, you will begin to hear people talking about *breadboards,* boards on which electronic circuitry are mounted in home workshops.

An almost perfect marriage has taken place between amateur radio hobbyists and personal computer hobbyists. In terms of cost, availability of supplies and materials, and compatibility with home workshops, the two areas are very much alike. Inevitably, a number of hobbyists have combined the two fields. Some have used their microcomputers to convert messages to and from Morse code, enabling the transmission of as many as a thousand words per minute. In other operations, the microcomputer takes the place of the human station operator. Using the radio, the computer establishes contact with another station, acknowledges responses, and even, supposedly, holds a "conversation" by playing prerecorded tapes. The purpose behind all of this escapes me. Apparently, it is little more than a contest to see which radio operator can make the most contacts in this manner. Well, we are talking about games, after all.

• Model Railroading

Many of the establishments along New York's Fifth Avenue seem to enjoy outdoing each other when it comes to window displays at Christmastime. Not long ago, the unofficial prize went to a window that was not on Fifth Avenue but a few feet in from the corner on a side street. Swissair, the airline company, had set up an Alpine village, complete with ski lift and perhaps a half-dozen tiny electric trains. Everything was in perfect scale, and those little trains went scooting and scurrying around the layout with the ceaseless determination of salmon swimming upstream. When one train stopped, another started. As one disappeared over a bridge, yet another emerged from a tunnel. Trains stopped at stations and freight yards, loading and unloading. Up hill and down dale came the little trains. Unfortunately, a great many children who wanted to see the display were unable to do so; much of the space in front of the window was occupied by adults, all male, shouldering and elbowing each other for a better view. Luckily, I had my two-year-old son with me. He expressed something less than enthusiasm for the arrangement, but it provided me with an excuse to get up front so that I could watch the whole operation.

Who can say why electric trains are so fascinating? If you are a railroad hobbyist, then you know your trains intrigue not only you, but just about anyone who sees them run. Imagine, if you can, the possibilities of a computerized train layout. Imagine running your

trains at varying speeds, opening and closing gates, synchronizing crossings, and even, if you have a sadistic bent, staging disasters.

If you need some link with reality, the next time you pass a freight yard or a railroad crossing, look for the particolored bars on the sides of the railroad cars. They constitute the input to the railroad companies' computer systems designed to keep track of the cars' whereabouts.

• Video Games

There is on the market a wide variety of games that can be played on a video screen simply by plugging them in to an ordinary television receiver. Court games (tennis, hockey, etc.), shooting-gallery games, and other diversions can be purchased in most department stores. It may be possible, with some minor adjustments, to use these games in conjunction with your CRT terminal instead of the family television set.

Other video games are programmed into the microcomputer. Some involve imaginary travels in outer space; one such game is based on the "Star Trek" television series.

Chess, checkers, and tic-tac-toe can also be played on video displays, as well as the so-called casino-type games—blackjack, poker, roulette, etc. (There is even blackjack software available for certain programmable calculators.)

A number of children's games are also available for programming into a microcomputer that uses a CRT display. Programs for virtually all of these games can be purchased at computer stores or by mail.

• Computerized Music

Whether computers are capable of making music depends upon whether you consider electronic tones to be musical notes. To most people, the term "electronic music" connotes a collection of blips and beeps in various frequencies, which, among other things, are not conducive to the listener's leaving a concert humming a tune. On the other hand, some of the finest music in the world has been performed using sounds that bear little or no resemblance to known musical instruments. (If you doubt that, then you have never heard a magnificent record called "Switched-On Bach," in which the music of Johann Sebastian Bach is played on a Moog synthesizer.)

Since music is a creative field, how you make music with a computer depends on your own creativity. For openers, you might want to interface a microcomputer with a small electric organ so that the computer rather than a person does the playing. There are also many sound synthesizers of various types, styles, and prices.

Your friendly neighborhood computer store or mail-order supplier undoubtedly has a "music board," available fully assembled or in kit form, that is either compatible with your computer or readily adaptable through an appropriate interface. These boards usually come complete with the necessary circuitry, a speaker, facilities for hooking up to an external audio system, and the ability to produce a surprisingly large repertoire of sounds.

Software for producing music is also available from computer stores and mail-order companies. Recently, some of the hobbyist magazines have been carrying programs for such classics as the works of Scott Joplin to be played by a computer.

The effect of electronic music is not necessarily unpleasant. Two of my favorite records are of George Gershwin's "Rhapsody in Blue." One is a reissue of a 1926 recording by the original Paul Whiteman orchestra, with the composer at the piano. The other, recorded in the mid-1970s, features a well-known pianist handling the solos, but all of the orchestral portions of the piece are played by a synthesizer, although it does not synthesize a single conventional musical instrument. The thing is full of *doits, bloops,* electronic *wah-wahs* and whistles. And I love it.

• Computerized Art

This is not the place to get into a discussion about what constitutes art. In this context, at least, consider the words "art" and "graphics" as interchangeable.

Computer art, as an art form, has gained some respectability, particularly among people in the computer field. Large- and medium-sized computers have been programmed to produce complex and rather attractive abstracts as well as representational works. For the time being, that seems to be beyond the scope of most microcomputers. Nevertheless, some forms of art or graphics are certainly possible now.

For example, you have probably seen commercial operations in which a subject places himself before a TV camera for a moment, a button is pushed, and a printer terminal then produces a "computerized photograph," comprised of a series of light and dark dots or, in some cases, lines or X's. A number of microcomputers can interface with a camera similar to the type used in these commercial operations, but the device is fairly expensive. At this writing, prices run around two hundred dollars for the camera in kit form, and about three hundred dollars assembled. In addition, it requires an interface, also available in either kit form or assembled, that costs about the same as the camera.

There are a number of graphic displays that can be programmed into the computer for use with an already existing CRT terminal or in conjunction with specially designed peripherals, including some employing color. There are also programs for producing graphics which permit the operator to make his own designs and compositions. A handy Polaroid camera makes the result permanent.

In all likelihood, the microcomputer you buy will have at least two or three games that are either part of the instruction manual or are available as optional extras for relatively nominal cost. If you enjoy playing games with your computer, the local computer store can provide you with manuals, programs, and even peripherals, specifically designed for diversion and amusement. But as you and your machine become more comfortable with each other, you will probably eventually rise to meet the ultimate challenge: creating your own games.

What could be more appropriate than to wish you good luck?

10

YOUR PERSONAL COMPUTER—
BUY OR BUILD?

There are two ways of having a microcomputer of your very own. One way is to go to a store, buy one, take it home and plug it in. The other way is to go to a store and purchase the necessary components for a microcomputer and begin putting it together yourself.

There are some compromises between these two extremes. For example, you may decide to purchase a fully operational microcomputer and one I/O device, and then build one or two or even several I/Os yourself. On the other hand, you may choose to do just the reverse: after putting together your own microcomputer, you may decide that a particular peripheral is too complicated or too time-consuming to be assembled piece by piece.

It is presumptuous for anyone to generalize about which method is better, because the decision is a highly individual one, based on several factors:

Finances. In every case, without exception, it is cheaper to build than it is to buy, all other things being equal. Certainly, buying a smaller or less powerful device may cost less than building a larger, more powerful one. ("Power" in this instance generally refers to a device's overall capabilities, including versatility and speed of operation.) In such cases, all other things are not equal.

Need. In the world of the hobbyist, particularly the computer hobbyist, "need" is difficult to define. It can be determined by the time-is-money principle, which means that even though it may cost more to buy a fully assembled unit, the time that you save will be put to more productive, money-producing use. Need can also refer to an intense yearning that cannot be satisfied except by buying the equipment that is your heart's desire.

Space. In addition to setting aside "living quarters" for your computer and its relatives, if you decide to build, you are going to need a work area that is clean, quiet, well lit, and relatively free of outside disturbances, such as curious children and spouses. If you do not have something resembling a workbench, it is probably best to forget about building.

Time. A hobby is a pastime. To pursue it, you must have the time to pass. Careful attention to detail is essential; you cannot rush electronic constructions. Furthermore, even the most skilled technicians sometimes make mistakes so that some tasks have to be done twice, perhaps even three or four times. If you decide to buy a kit and do not have a specific time period set aside to work on it, it will gather dust and obsolescence on a shelf until you get around to it—if, indeed, you ever do.

Temperament. Unquestionably, this is the most important factor to consider in deciding whether to buy a microcomputer system or to build one. What is needed if you decide to build, is patience, some manual dexterity, a mechanical/technological inclination, and a genuine feeling that getting in there among all those wires, leads, transistors, chips, pins, boards, etc., is something that is a source of genuine enjoyment and pleasure. If you can take it or leave it, chances are you will leave it. If you harbor an active dislike for such things, your money will be put to better use if you donate it to some charity, preferably one devoted to helping people who suffer from nervous breakdowns.

• Who Makes What?

Up to now, I have made only vague references to manufacturers of microcomputers, peripherals, and software. With one or two exceptions, I have carefully refrained from mentioning names (except for illustrative purposes). That practice will be continued in this chapter. To begin with, the mention of a specific product or manufacturer in a book like this carries with it an implied endorsement, no matter how many disclaimers to the contrary are made. Because it is impossible to be fully acquainted with all the products of all manufacturers, let alone have a comprehensive knowledge of reliability and capability, it is best to avoid such implied endorsements. Furthermore, and perhaps more important, the microcomputer industry is (to use a favorite industry word) volatile. There is every reason to believe that microcomputers will closely follow a pattern established by the calculator and digital watch industries. Many companies, large and small, rushed into the marketplace with hand-held calculators and digital watches. Soon there were mergers. Soon after that, there were inventory problems caused by shifts in the economy, daring mar-

keting strategies on the part of certain aggressive firms, and production innovations that enabled some companies to price their products far below those of their competitors. Before long, some companies went bankrupt and others simply backed out of the calculator and watch business. That industry now seems to have stabilized, but similar stabilization in the microcomputer industry is several years away. Already, however, several firms involved in the manufacture of microcomputer components have been reported to be on shaky ground. Other companies have begun to merge; whether that is an indication of strength or weakness is difficult to ascertain without probing into the companies' histories.

More important for the consumer, however, is the fact that any product, system, or device (with the possible exception of software) that is mentioned specifically is in danger of becoming obsolete. A good example is the prepackaged, self-contained microcomputer system that sells for well under a thousand dollars and which can be unwrapped, plugged in, and put to work. At this writing, there are four or five such units on the market. But there seems little doubt throughout the microcomputer industry that this will change and that soon the consumer will be able to choose from among many microcomputer systems selling for around five hundred dollars. As chip technology continues to advance along with production techniques, there is every reason to believe that the price of such self-contained units will go down even more.

Rather than recommend or suggest or even mention specific products, therefore, I would urge you to visit a nearby computer store. You may wind up buying your computer from a local department store or from one of the major mail-order catalog retailers. Nevertheless, you should visit a computer store, anyway. You will have an opportunity to look at the very latest equipment, and possibly, under close supervision, you will have a chance to play with the machines. Because of the nature of microcomputing, the state of the art, and the appeal that it has to devoted hobbyists, browsers who ask a lot of questions are not tolerated in computer stores, they are expected. It's a good place, therefore, to obtain a basic education about what is available at the time you are ready to buy. Chances are also excellent that you will come home with an armload of lavishly produced literature, some of which may prove to be beyond your comprehension. Still, the pamphlets, brochures, and catalogs will allow you to become more familiar with available equipment.

• Buying a System

There is no escaping the fact that a modicum of technology is involved, no matter what kind of system you eventually decide upon. After all, you are going to have to learn how to operate the thing. The purveyor of one such system declares in its brochure that "No previous knowledge of computers or programming is needed!" But the fact remains that the system comes equipped with a three-hundred-page instruction and programming manual, and anyone who buys the system is going to have to read that manual, or at least portions of it.

Still, the chief advantage of a plug-in, ready-to-go system is that the user does not have to fool with wiring, circuitry, or anything else that comprises the innards of the machinery.

The complete systems generally come equipped with important and useful ancillaries, available as "standard equipment" or as "optionals." Thus, one unit that is sold as a complete system includes the computer, a built-in keyboard, a 12-inch video display, and a cassette recorder. The supplier throws in a cassette carrying programs for blackjack and backgammon, and, of course, a fairly hefty owner's manual. The system includes 4K of ROM (read-only memory) and 4K of RAM (random-access memory). The memory can be expanded without peripheral equipment to a total capability of 62K, and there are I/O ports for even more memory, which can be added as needed or desired. There are also ports for other peripherals, and the company promises to have available a low-priced printer fully compatible with the system. At this time, programs for payrolls, personal finances, kitchen use, and teaching arithmetic are available. Further expansions are promised and include floppy-disk storage capability and units that will make it possible to have access to the computer via telephone lines. The company literature suggests that graphics, music synthesizers, security systems, and home environment systems can be designed by the owner for use in conjunction with this system. Other manufacturers offer similar prospects for their systems.

When one considers that a complete microcomputer system is available for about the cost of a good color television set or a medium-to-good stereo system, the prefabricated computer would seem to have enormous appeal. There are, however, certain drawbacks. One of the things you should look for when buying a complete system is the accessibility of other equipment. You might begin by purchasing a basic unit—say, the computer, a video terminal with keyboard, and a cassette recorder. Now, if in six months, you decide to expand that system, either through the addition of memory or other peripherals, you may discover that you are locked in to the devices made by the manufacturer of the basic system. Despite the fact that other peripherals may be cheaper or more suited to your specific needs, you may not be able to use them. It is important, therefore, to know whether your system can interface with other peripherals. If it cannot, you may have good reasons for buying it anyway—price, size, immediate need, etc.— but at least you should know where you stand.

Commodore's PET preassembled computer system.
The entire system is contained in this tabletop unit,
including keyboard, video screen and, at lower left,
a tape cassette I/O device. Courtesy Commodore.

A related problem has to do with the ability to "crawl inside the box." Chances are that if you decide to purchase a complete system, you have no desire to get involved in the electronics of that system, but if you later change your mind and feel like performing a little surgery on the computer (transplants, implants, amputations, corrective surgery, etc.), the construction of the components of the system may thwart your passion. Should you decide to make your own repairs, your frustration may be profound indeed.

● **Building Your Own**

In my opinion, microcomputer kits can be readily sorted into two categories: one category consists of ludicrously simple kits which provide little more than amusement and are designed primarily for children. The other category includes all other kits.

Make no mistake: if you are a raw beginner with no background or experience in electronics, putting together a microcomputer kit will, to put it mildly, not be easy. But if you are prepared to face that fact with the philosophy that life, after all, is not easy, then there are certain practical and emotional satisfactions to be gained by building your own computer. (Please note: the assumption from the outset is that such building involves the assembly of prepackaged kits. If it is your desire or intention to begin building from scratch, you have no business reading this book.)

One of the satisfactions to be derived from assembling a kit is the direct personal involvement, the sense of accomplishment that comes with a job well done. Of course, the sense of frustration that comes with a job *not* done is —to borrow a word from the industry— programmed into the process. Apart from providing some ego massage, however, kit building enables you to gain an intimate knowledge of the insides of a computer. Everything you read is essentially abstract, no matter how proficient you may be at conceptualizing in your mind. It cannot compare with actually putting the bits and pieces together so that they work. Another satisfaction, a very concrete one, is the fact, as stated earlier, that without exception the cost of a kit is less than the cost of an assembled unit, all other things being equal. You can save a lot of money by building from kits, but it will cost you a lot of time.

If you become really expert at putting together and taking apart the various elements of your computer, you can make that machine and its peripherals dance to just about any tune you care to play. That electronic servant that is the focal point of so many science fiction stories is within the realm of your reality when and if you become a computer expert. You cannot become such an expert unless you are prepared to "make" the machine yourself.

● **Types of Kits**

A number of so called "trainer" kits are on the market and are available for relatively low cost. Their main purpose is to acquaint the purchaser with microcomputers. They offer a good introduction to microprocessing, provided, however, that the instructions and other information packed with the kits are complete and are understandable to the purchaser. Many of these kits are intended for people who have some background in electronics or computers.

Generally, trainer kits can be played with so that the user can see how they operate and function. They can even be changed to show what happens when there are variations in the configurations of circuitry. They are, however, rather limited, and once the education process is over, there is not much that can be done with the equipment because most of these kits have no provisions either for additional memory or for peripherals.

If you are considering the purchase of a training kit, *first look at the instructions*. If they are not perfectly clear to you, disregard any of the other advantages or disadvantages the kit may have.

The second thing to look for is whether the kit provides for additional memory and peripherals. Some of the newer kits make it possible to hook up the-assembled machine to other manufacturers' devices as one's interest in microcomputers grows.

Beyond the trainer kits, there are a great many products that vary in complexity, so-

The IMSAI PCS-80/30 microcomputer. Its cover has
been removed to show the innards. This is one of
the many units available in kit form or fully assembled.
Courtesy IMSAI.

phistication, and price. Among the things to look for in such kits is the relative ease with which circuit boards can be inserted and removed, and which do not require particularly exotic parts. Perhaps the first ˉpractical personal computer was the Altair, manufactured by MITS, Inc. of Albuquerque, New Mexico. (MITS has since merged with Pertec Computer Corporation.) The Altair was designed with peripherals and accessories in mind. As a result, MITS also developed what came to be known as the "Altair bus." (You may recall that a bus is a group of conductors used to transmit data from one part of the system to another.) The Altair S-100 bus, while not exactly a standard, has enjoyed considerable popularity. If, therefore, a kit uses or is compatible with an S-100 bus, your chances of hooking up with a variety of peripherals are quite good.

It has been implied—but perhaps, for the record, I should now point out directly—that virtually anything that can be made part of a microcomputer system can be purchased in kit form, from the basic computer to all of the peripherals. There are even calculator kits. If you become really adept at, and enthusiastic over, putting it all together yourself, you may find yourself wandering away from the computer store to indulge in some expensive browsing through the catalogs and retail outlets of the better electronic supply houses.

• Secondhand Equipment

Although there is certainly never a guarantee of a steady supply of used computer equipment, invariably there is something available most of the time. Generally, such availability arises from the usual reasons for secondhand items becoming available in any hobby: some people become emotionally, intellectually, or financially unwilling to continue supporting their hobby and are willing to dispose of all of its appurtenances. (More than one about-to-

be married enthusiast has heard the cry: "Either that stuff goes, or I do." Invariably, the "stuff," being unable to satisfy certain basic human passions, is sacrificed.) Then, there are always the gadget-happy who believe that newer and bigger is better, so existing equipment is constantly being replaced by the latest innovations. The result is a lively trade in computers, peripherals, and accessories.

There are good reasons for buying used equipment, too. The first consideration, of course, is price, although it is always best to weigh the cost of a piece of used equipment against the cost of the same equipment purchased new. Microcomputers represent an area of merchandising with somewhat erratic discount patterns, and the difference between new and used equipment may not be very great. Another good reason for buying used equipment is the unwillingness to purchase a kit and build the item yourself. Not every kit is necessarily available in assembled form except when it has been assembled by another purchaser who has then decided, for whatever reason, to dispose of it.

Sometimes, in their enthusiasm to plunge into the marketplace, manufacturers promote equipment which is in short supply. Actual production may even be held up pending sufficient advance orders to warrant a production run. A microcomputer owner who wants or needs a piece of equipment immediately may be able to avoid the delay caused by such practices and be satisfied with a secondhand product. Conversely, there are those who delight in working with obsolete equipment that is no longer in production. Tinkerers who enjoy rebuilding antiques have no choice but to buy secondhand merchandise.

Because of the relatively few moving parts in a microcomputer, computing equipment is subject to very little wear. Tear, however, is another matter. The efficiency and durability of a piece of used equipment depend very little on how *much* it was used and very much on how *well* it was used. If and when used equipment breaks down, it is usually because it was not well put together in the first place or because it was subject to abuse and/or negligent maintenance. Therefore, never buy used equipment without first checking it out carefully. If you make your purchase by mail, make sure the supplier offers a money-back guarantee and get it in writing.

Used equipment can often be purchased at your local computer store, although availability tends to vary not only with the whims of original owners, but with the type of store. The periodicals listed in the Bibliography carry advertisements for used computer equipment. One of the best sources of used equipment is the local computer club. The informality and camaraderie typical of such groups are highly conducive to fair and honorable exchanges.

● **Tools of the Trade**

No true gadget-lover ever has enough tools. Lovers of electronic gadgets are particularly fond of things that light up, that cause arrows to bounce up and down dials and that emit clicks, crackles, and whistles. Many microcomputers and peripherals provide for the testing of signals and voltage to determine whether the device has been properly assembled and is operating as it should. Typically, such tests require the application of an oscilloscope or a multimeter, neither of which is cheap or likely to be lying around the shop of someone who does not usually work with electronics. If you do not own the necessary testing devices, you will undoubtedly find it possible to borrow them if you belong to a computer club. You may be able to borrow or rent them from a computer store. Certainly, you will have no difficulty in buying them.

Just how fancy a set of tools you want to own depends, of course, on you. Listed below are the tools that are considered essential, presented in descending order of importance. What you buy beyond these is between you and your conscience.

Soldering iron. If you do not own a soldering iron, buy one when you get your kit; it will be impossible to put the kit together without it. Make sure that the soldering iron has a fairly sharp point, and unless you are gifted with a delicate touch, get a light-duty, low-wattage model. There are two kinds of solder, but as far as putting together a computer kit is concerned, there is only one kind—thin, fine solder with a rosin core. (The other kind has an acid core. If you use this type, you will damage the equipment and void the warranty that comes with your kit.)

Screwdrivers. In addition to the standard-size screwdrivers found in most household tool kits, you should have a set of small screwdrivers. These are often sold in relatively inexpensive prepackaged sets in graduated sizes. Your screwdrivers should include at least one large one and one small one suitable for Phillips-head screws. (Incidentally, even if you decide not to build your own kits after all, you will find these little screwdrivers very handy around the house for all kinds of small work, such as simple jewelry repair, changing watchbands, tightening loose screws on tape recorders, etc.)

Pliers. You probably already have a pair of conventional pliers for tightening nuts. These will be needed for mounting various pieces of hardware on your computer's metal chassis. In addition, a pair of long-nose pliers will prove useful for holding small parts while soldering them into place. And, like the small screwdrivers, long-nosed pliers justify their existence by performing a number of little tasks totally unrelated to computers.

Cutters. You will probably have to trim and shape pieces of metal, and sharp diagonal cutters will come in handy.

Brushes. Several small, soft brushes will go a long way toward making your work easier, because they can keep the immediate area in which you are working free of dust, scraps, and debris. If you own a portable typewriter, chances are it came equipped with such a brush. Fine artists' paint brushes, which have either been cleaned or never used, are also adequate. But perhaps the handiest and least expensive brush is a used toothbrush. (Obviously, once it moves from the bathroom to the workbench, the toothbrush should never again return to the bathroom.)

Pointed tool. I know that is not an official or technical designation, but what I mean is something that will enable you to make small, clean holes. An awl is probably the best.

Magnifier. A magnifying glass is recommended for checking soldered points to make sure that there have been no dribbles of liquid solder which can cause short-circuiting. You may even find it easier to do the actual soldering under magnification. There are several devices that will enable you to do so, including a magnifying lens mounted on a stand. My particular favorite, however, is a jeweler's loupe, particularly the kind that can be easily mounted onto an eyeglass frame. A very good loupe with two lenses—providing three different strengths of magnification—can be purchased for under fifteen dollars and, like other tools mentioned here, earns its price in doing double and triple service around the house. I use mine for making repairs on small objects and for inspecting photographic negatives.

Receptacles. A kit contains a number of very small parts that should be checked against the parts list before you begin to work. As you do so, the parts should be separated by type and placed in small, temporary containers. If you should misplace one of those parts, your attempts at finding it again may make you a candidate for a padded room. By placing those parts in the receptacles, you can save both the part and your sanity. Almost anything will do—whiskey jiggers, small paper cups, clean ashtrays, etc.

Assorted screws, nuts, and bolts. It is probably a good idea to lay in a small supply of these—although, if you are like me, you will discover that you have all the sizes and shapes available except the one you need at the moment.

Storage bins. Arrange for some more-or-less permanent storage areas for the various parts and materials. Most hardware supply stores carry small plastic boxes or trays that are suitable for such purposes. Recycled baby-food jars make excellent storage containers.

Wire. The retailer who supplies your kit should also be able to supply spools of wire with color-coded insulation. The wire is not expensive and is backup material that is worth having.

Tape. Certainly your household toolbox contains a spool of electrical tape. If it does not, get some, even if you do not plan to build a computer.

Tubing. There is a type of plastic tubing that shrinks when exposed to a little heat. This is available in various sizes and will prove very useful in forming tight connections.

Labels. Your storage bins most certainly should be labeled. You may also want to label drawers, cabinets, places on a pegboard designated for a specific use, etc. The labeling technique you use is a matter of personal taste. I prefer the kind of plastic tape on which letters are embossed by passing the tape through a small embossing machine. These devices range in price from a dollar or two on up. The more expensive the embosser, the more elegant it is. I have never found much use for the elegance, so I recommend that you get the cheapest label embosser you can find.

It goes without saying (but I will say it, nevertheless) that adequate lighting is essential. If you do not have a good strong lamp for your workbench, consider the possibility of the so called "architect's lamp." This type of lamp can best be described by comparing it to a human arm. The "shoulder" of the lamp is its base, and most models are available with a clamp so that they can be screwed to the edge of a table or desk. The "arm" pivots at that base so that the lamp can be moved anywhere. The "arm" has a kind of "elbow" in the middle so that the lamp can be moved up and down with ease. At the "wrist," the lamp housing itself is mounted. This too swivels and pivots. Thus, the light can be brought as close as necessary, high or low, and can easily be swung out of the way when it is not wanted. An arrangement of springs makes the lamp stay put. Prices for these lamps start at about twenty dollars. The higher-priced lamps have nothing to offer but styling, and I have yet to see a sixty- or seventy-dollar architect's lamp that functions better than a twenty-dollar one.

Recently, a technique called *"wire wrapping"* has appeared on the scene. It involves a method of making efficient temporary connections, necessary when working with experimental circuitry or making temporary hookups. Wire wrapping eliminates the need of soldering and unsoldering, but it does require special connectors and sockets, as well as some specialized but relatively inexpensive tools. Most computer-store personnel can discuss wire wrapping and provide the necessary tools and materials.

● **Where to Buy Your Computer**

As this is being written, extensive plans are afoot for marketing complete, self-contained, ready-to-plug-in-and-go computer systems in conventional retail outlets. You can probably buy a microcomputer in a department store, from one of the giant mail-order catalog firms, at appliance dealers, and from retailers of hi-fi stereo equipment. You probably know from experience which are your favorite merchants, the ones that offer the best prices, the best

service, and the greatest reliability. It would be easy to name several nationally known retailers who merchandise many products under their own brand names. Some we can swear by; others we would swear at.

But the advent of microcomputers for personal use has brought with it a whole new industry, not only in terms of manufacturing, but in terms of retailing as well. The first practical personal computer appeared on the scene in the mid-1970s. Within a year or two a phenomenon called the computer store popped up in cities all over the country. There are independent dealers, chains, and franchises. Some of them—indeed, most of them—are run by dedicated souls who are in the business as much for the fun of it as for the money. Others are run by nitwits or charlatans. As mentioned earlier, the microcomputer industry is a highly volatile one. No doubt the structure of computer retailing will change somewhat. But for the moment, at least, there are computer stores all over the place, and for those who do not have access to such establishments, there are more than enough mail-order companies anxious to separate you from your money. (See Appendix III.)

Despite the fact that home computers may be available from tried and tested retailers such as department stores, it is highly recommended that if you have access to a computer store, you go and pay a visit. For one thing, a well-stocked store is likely to have enough equipment on display for you to see and operate the units that are of most interest to you. A computer store is also likely to have a number of peripherals and other accessories that you may want to consider. Most important, the proprietor or clerk who waits on you in a computer store is almost certain to be far more knowledgeable about computers than a sales clerk in a department store. If you do business with the computer store, chances are excellent that you will be able to telephone from time to time with a question or a problem and get a prompt response. In many cases, a computer store is also a kind of informal clubhouse where computerniks gather, ostensibly to make a purchase or look at new equipment. Invariably, however, discussions and conversations take place. Dede Veit, the wife of Stanley Veit, proprietor of the Computer Mart of New York, works in the store when she is not teaching school. "There is no such thing as a typical customer," Dede once told me. "They come in all sizes, shapes, colors, nationalities, and interest levels. We get the local nut who comes in, stands around and reads all the magazines. His concept of a computer is a calculator that he holds in his hands. And then we get people from IBM, people who design, build, and run these things. And it runs the full gamut in between . . ."

Those magazines, by the way, are important. I shall have more to say about books and magazines in the Bibliography, but one of the chief advantages in dealing with a computer store is that you can pick up and look through many books and publications to see which ones are best suited for your needs. The same, not incidentally, is true of kits. Shopping at a computer store gives you the opportunity to read the material accompanying the kit to determine whether it makes sense to you.

Most computer-store owners are capable of making repairs and adjustments on the equipment they sell. Understandably, however, they prefer to devote as little time as possible to such activities and are therefore likely to carry equipment that will not only keep the customers happy but will keep the dealers relatively free to invest their time in more profit-generating endeavors. One can generally trust the equipment sold at computer stores.

An alternative to the computer store is the mail-order supplier. I am reluctant to recommend mail-order purchases of computer equipment, not because of the companies offering these services—most of them are quite reliable—but because it is often difficult to determine, without actually laying on hands, the ease with which a piece of equipment can be operated, its compatibility with already owned equipment, and the full extent of its limits and capabilities.

If you find it necessary to deal with mail-order firms, try to get as much detailed information in advance as you possibly can. Ask questions by mail or telephone. Describe the system now in use to which you plan to add the new equipment under consideration. Find out what the company's return policy is.

It is a popular conceit to refer to microcomputers as "low cost," but that is a relative term. Compared to an automobile or a full-sized computer, microcomputers are low cost. Compared to a transistor radio or a package of chewing gum, their cost is enormous. The point is that purchasing a microcomputer involves the expenditure of a decent enough sum so that if you are planning to spend that money with a retailer you have never heard of or done business with before, it will do no harm to check with the Better Business Bureau, the Consumer Affairs unit of your state Attorney General's office, and the local district office of the Federal Trade Commission to see what, if anything, they know about the dealer who wants your money.

● **Checklist**

You have decided that you want to buy a microcomputer. You have probably narrowed down your choices to two or three models and now have to decide which is best for you. This checklist should help you make that decision. I have attempted to arrange the items on this list in what I consider descending order of importance; however, your own needs and preferences are your best guide. It is conceivable, for example, that the amount of noise a microcomputer makes is more important in some circumstances than what the computer costs. So you should probably consider all of the points in the checklist, but not necessarily in the order in which they are given.

1. Ease of operation. Whether the computer you buy is simple to operate because you prefer that, or difficult and complicated because you like challenges, should probably be the most important factor in determining what unit you buy. Regardless of what the clerk or dealer tells you about any given unit, ask to see the instruction manual that comes with it. If the manual is not within the realm of your ready comprehension, give some serious second thoughts about buying that particular unit. This is especially important as far as kits are concerned.

2. Cost. You already know what price range the equipment under consideration falls in and whether you can pay that price. But there are two important factors which should also be considered in determining cost. First, how much will it cost for the peripherals and accessories that you now want to add to your unit? Second, assuming you have in mind the ultimate utilization of a larger and more complex system based on the microcomputer you are now buying, what will it cost for that complete system?

3. I/O devices. Is the imput device one that you can easily handle? You may want a typewriter-like keyboard, or you may feel that the calculator-type keypad is sufficient for your needs. Similarly, the output can range from a display of LEDs (light emitting diodes; similar to a display of a hand-held calculator), a video display, or a printer. Regardless of what you plan to use in the future, you should make sure that the unit you are buying has the I/O capability that you want right now.

4. Built-in memory. It is difficult to establish a criterion for built-in memory because that depends so much on the needs of the user. In general, however, a machine that offers 32K of memory will probably be sufficient for most needs.

5. Removable RAM. To permit expansion of the system, a microcomputer should be able to accommodate a reasonable quantity of removable random-access memory (RAM). "Reasonable" is whatever you decide it is.

6. Software. The microcomputer should have as "standard equipment" either software or "firmware" to enable the machine to run. Ideally, the package should also include at least one applications program, even if it is only a game-playing one, so that you can get the machine doing things immediately. Also, make sure that there is enough software available, perhaps as optional extras, for your immediate specific needs and purposes. Programs that permit the saving or filing of data are essential for applications beyond game-playing or one-time calculations.

A system from a reliable manufacturer who promises to supply additional software packages in the foreseeable future has much to recommend it.

7. Mass Storage. Determine the types of mass storage—disk, floppy disk, magnetic tape cassettes—that can be easily interfaced with the microcomputer under consideration. For purposes of economy and relative simplicity, the ability to interface with a cassette-type tape recorder is a definite plus.

8. Adaptability and expansion. If you have a specific job or group of jobs in mind for a microcomputer, it is obviously pointless to purchase a machine that is incapable of performing those tasks or of being easily adapted for the purposes you need. Similarly, it is almost certain that you will not be forever satisfied with the unit you buy now. Once you begin to operate it and you and your computer get to know each other, you will surely want to expand your horizons and its capability. A microprocessing system that is incapable of such expansion is not a worthwhile investment.

On the other hand, if you plan to *dedicate* your computer—that is, assign it to one or two specific tasks and use it for no other—

then versatility and expandability are features you may be paying for and never have an opportunity to use.

9. Programming. Early on, find out what language your computer speaks. Machine language, you will recall, is the most "powerful" (i.e. able to make the most proficient use of the computer's memory), and high-level language—probably BASIC, a version thereof, or something similar to it—is the easiest to deal with. You should know what language your computer speaks, what language it is capable of "learning" through the use of assemblers and/or compilers, the ease or difficulty of programming in your computer's language(s), and what software is already available in your computer's language(s).

10. Reputation. If you are purchasing a system that has been on the market for some time, it will require only a little detective work to find out whether experts consider that system to be reliable. Talk to the people at the computer store and, even if you do not plan to join the group, write or telephone the president of the nearest computer society. If, however, the system or piece of equipment is fairly new on the market, then you will have to rely on the reputation of its manufacturer. If the firm is readily recognizable to you, you should have no difficulty in making the decision pro or con. If you do not know the company, again, people in a computer store or a nearby computer club should be able to help you. Do not be swayed by outward appearances and by what computerniks like to call "bells and whistles." If a machine is manufactured by the Fly-by-Night Electronics Company, with corporate headquarters in the Fiji Islands, you should think twice about buying it, no matter how pretty it is.

11. Future products. The easiest and most pleasant way to expand a computer system is to add on peripherals made specifically for that purpose by the manufacturer of the original system. Most manufacturers of computer systems happily trumpet their plans for devices which expand and enhance their system. If the literature describing a microcomputer that you have in mind doesn't include such boasting, you had better find out whether the system will accept products made by other companies.

12. Maintenance and repairs. Discuss with the dealer the availability of maintenance and repair service. Your unit may come with the best service warranty ever written for a product anywhere in the world, but if you have to pack up the machine and ship it halfway across the country in order to have it fixed, that warranty is of little use to you. Quality of service is also important. I could easily incur a lawsuit by naming a very well-known electronics manufacturer which makes superb products but whose so-called factory service has done more harm than good. I have actually gotten back a product from their service shop in worse shape than it was when I brought it in. Many microcomputer systems are *modular,* which means that they consist of modules, best described as kinds of building blocks which fit together with other building blocks to make a whole. Such units are easier to repair and maintain because the modules can be removed and worked on.

13. Physical characteristics. Check out the size and appearance of the unit you want to buy. If it is in kit form, take a good look at pictures of the finished product. I suppose the appearance of a microcomputer does not have to please you esthetically, but somehow, considering the time, money, care, and devotion invested in it, it ought to. Appearance aside, its size is important because it will have to fit into whatever space you allocate for it. Furthermore, some peripherals can be rather noisy. A typewriter-like printer or a Teletypewriter can set up a considerable racket. That may be a factor you will want to consider.

14. The dealer. If the dealer offering to sell

you a computer is uncommunicative, unknowledgeable, condescending, or surly, take your business elsewhere. No matter how much you know or learn about microcomputers, you are going to have questions, and many of these questions can only be answered by the dealer. Furthermore, he should be willing, within reason, to make limited repairs and adjustments and to help you with questions and problems that arise after you buy your equipment. If you have any doubts about a dealer's ability or willingness to be co-operative and helpful, check him out with the local computer club. Often, a computer club can make or break a computer store.

• Maintenance

Above all, keep your computer clean. Remember that a microcomputer consists of myriad intricate circuits, some of which are nearly microscopic in size. You can imagine, therefore, the havoc that can be wreaked by a speck of dust, a careless cigarette or cigar ash, a crumb of food, or spilled liquid. That doesn't mean that if a caraway seed from your ham-and-cheese-on-rye drops into the computer your system will break down. It does mean, however, that a reasonable amount of care should be taken to keep foreign materials away from the system. When you buy a computer, buy or make dust covers for it at the same time.

If you plan to get your hands into the machine itself either by building kits or by adding circuitry, it is probably a good idea to keep the working computer some little distance from your workbench. Tiny screws, drops of solder, and bits of wire—all of which are capable of creating short circuits—can cause you hours of frustrated searching trying to discover what has gone wrong.

It is not unusual to see a home computer standing there with its innards on display. In all cases, but especially when a system is being worked on, the microcomputer should be kept in a place inaccessible to children who are not in the company of adults. Even many adults cannot resist the temptation of turning on the computer and watching it light up. That may be all right with a self-contained, completely covered system, but such curiosity should be discouraged when it concerns a computer that has been or is being assembled by the operator.

Obviously, many peripherals can be turned on or off by their own switches. Often these switches are inadvertently left on for long periods of time. This is not only an unnecessary drain on power, but in some instances—for example, with some electric typewriters—parts may burn out. It is a good idea, therefore, to have the entire system wired to a main switch which must be turned on before the computer is used and turned off when the user is finished.

In general, your computer should reside in a quiet, clean, traffic-free location. The quiet enables the operator to concentrate on what he is doing; computers don't make very much noise. Sometimes a very low hum can be detected and, on occasion, ventilating fans may create a little more noise; rarely are these disturbing to other people. Some printers, particularly Teletypewriters, can, however, be quite noisy.

Certain types of computer memory are *volatile,* which means that they are automatically erased when the power is turned off. There are two ways of avoiding such a contingency. One is to leave the computer on all the time. In most small systems, the amount of power used if that is done is surprisingly low. A computer hobbyist I know worked out the costs of leaving his computer on all the time. He lives in New York City, which probably has the highest utility rates in the country. He calculated that providing continuous power to his system would cost twelve dollars a month.

Most systems will accommodate backup battery packs so that portions of the system can be left on.

A simpler method, or course, is to remove the data from volatile memory and store it on tape or on a disk.

• But How Much Does It Cost?

There are a number of factors involved in determining the exact cost of your microcomputer. Obviously, capability, in terms of the system's versatility and the size of its memory, is an important consideration. But there are others.

Typically, cost to most people means the price you pay for what you get. However, there may be other factors worth considering. For example, there is the question of availability. The computer you want may be selling at a price that you consider a bargain. But if you have to wait three or four months (the situation that exists at this writing with one highly touted and well-advertised microcomputer system), you may prefer paying a little more or even a lot more money to get a machine immediately, particularly if you plan to use it for business applications. The additional cost might be rationalized by the time and money to be saved by obtaining the equipment earlier.

Another way of looking at cost has to do with how the equipment is to be used. If, for example, your computer will consist of nothing more than a diversion for you, whether you use it to play games or as a hobby, then cost becomes a function of self-indulgence. Certainly, games can be played with low-cost computers. Better games can be played more easily with higher-cost systems. As for the hobby aspects of it, we probably both know hobbyists perfectly content with equipment worth a couple of hundred dollars, and others who already own two or three thousand dollars' worth of equipment and are constantly looking for additions and accessories.

Yet, another and quite important consideration when determining the cost of your computer derives from the number of applications for which the computer will be used. If you decide to buy a system that costs a thousand dollars, then, stated simply, you have a thousand-dollar system. If, however, you use it to fulfill two ongoing functions, then it may be said that each function costs five hundred dollars. If you use it for a hundred ongoing functions, then each function costs only ten dollars.

EPILOGUE

Even the future is not what it used to be.

Paul Ambroise Valéry (1871–1945),
French poet and critic

As we approach the conclusion of this book, you may have a sense of dissatisfaction, a feeling that something is missing. Perhaps you have stayed with me this long in the hope that by the time you reached this point, you would know, first, whether a microcomputer is for you, and second, if it is, which one to go out and buy. As to the first, however, it is a decision only you can make. For a lot of people, it is not even a decision that can be made on the basis of rational thinking. If you, like me, are an inveterate gadget-lover, you will already have decided that you want a microcomputer; all that remains is to come up with one or two reasons to justify your decision to those who you feel require such justification. As to the second, any book that gets down to specific types and brands is, at best, useless, and at worst, doing the reader a disservice. Since not everyone's needs or desires are the same, a book like this can only generalize. Furthermore, any book that discusses specific microcomputers by name and model number is obsolete the moment it rolls off the presses. Changes in microcomputers are occurring almost daily. Significantly, those changes involve not only improvements in production,

developments in marketing and pricing, and totally new devices; they involve the attitudes people have toward computers.

Once thought of as a mysterious collection of wires, tapes, and blinking lights set up somewhere in an inaccessible ivory tower, computers have actually entered the home. Anyone with the space to hold an electric typewriter on a stand has the space to accommodate a computer. Already, large computers are "talking" to each other through the use of *modems* (an acronym for *mo*dulator/*dem*odulator), a device which permits an interchange between computers through the use of ordinary telephone lines. At present, few hobbyists are using modems, but it is only a question of time before they become more popular.

Some observers are predicting a totally computerized society. Through the use of modems, it should be possible to hook up your telephone to your computer, dial a central number, and have the news of the day printed out on your CRT terminal. Items that you want to save will be easily transmitted to hard copy. Other predictions are that, through the use of the telephone, your computer will be told by a supermarket's computer what is on sale today and at what price. You will then be able to tell the supermarket's computer what you want and, within a short time, your groceries will be delivered. Payment is simple enough. You simply give the supermarket's computer the number of your account at the local bank. The store's computer notifies the bank's computer of the amount of your order, and funds are transferred from your account to the store's account. (This is known as EFTS—Electronic Funds Transfer System—and has already been tried experimentally in several communities.)

If these scenarios seem far-fetched to you, don't tell that to the British Post Office.

In Britain, the post office runs the telephone system. Authorities have announced their intention of initiating, on an experimental basis, a service called Viewdata. The post office was expected to persuade approximately a thousand householders to purchase color TV sets equipped with Viewdata decoders, a calculator-type of keypad, and a modem for making contact with a data base by telephone. Viewdata is expected to supply such long-term information as telephone directory listings, travel timetables, financial data, tax advice, etc. It is possible that it will also offer information that is more current and subject to change, such as news headlines, weather, sports results, etc. "Behind it all," claims the distinguished British magazine *New Scientist,* "lies the post office's determination to get a better return on its enormous investment on copper buried underground—in other words, it wants to sell you more telephone calls." Americans who have had to deal with our own telephone system know all about aggressive marketing intended to encourage us to make more telephone calls; a version of Britain's Viewdata in the United States is certainly in the foreseeable future.

What else is in the foreseeable future? With computers in the home, it is possible that more people will have greater access to higher levels of education. In particular, the young, the aging, and the physically handicapped will have doors opened to them that heretofore have been closed. Alan C. Kay, principal scientist and head of the Learning Research Group of the Xerox Palo Alto Research Center, wrote in *Scientific American* (September 1977):

> The future increase in capacity and decrease in cost of microelectronic devices will not only give rise to compact and powerful hardware but also bring qualitative changes in the way human beings and computers interact. In the 1980s both adults and children will be able to have as personal possession a computer about the size of a large notebook with power to handle virtually all of their information and related needs. Computing and storage capacity will be many times that of current microcomputers. Tens of millions of basic operations per second will manipulate the equivalent of several thousand printed pages of information . . . The microelectronic revolution of the 1970s will bring about the personal computer of the 1980s, with sufficient storage and speed to support high-level computer languages and interacting graphic displays.

Dr. Kay further predicts that microcomputers will be in common use by physicians, composers, educators, homemakers, and school children. "Businessmen," he claims, "should have an active briefcase that contains a working simulation of their company."

Well, then what is one to do? To begin with, this book has not advised you on specifics. Furthermore, even if it had, such advice would have been useless because, by the time you get ready to go shopping, there will be changes and innovations. In any case, why not wait? Prices are certain to come down, computers are sure to become smaller and increasingly easier to operate. Why even think of buying a computer now?

The answer to that question lies within the

very center of your philosophy of life. It is wrong to say that computers are changing the way we live. They have already done so. Throughout history, only a few innovations have changed the status of humankind. One was the invention of writing. Another was the invention of printing. A third was the invention of computers. It is an ongoing, dynamic, and exciting process. You have the choice of observing it or participating in it.

It has always seemed to me that participants get more out of life than observers.

GLOSSARY

This glossary serves two purposes. First, it is, I hope, a handy reference for the terminology that appears throughout this book. Its second aim, however, is to acquaint you with computer terminology that you are likely to encounter when reading about computers or talking to people involved with them. Included are a number of terms that are not strictly applicable to microcomputers but which are so common in computerese that they are worth knowing.

This glossary, then, is a quick and handy dictionary (but by no means the best one; see Bibliography). But don't confine its use to reference purposes. Start with the first entry and read through the glossary once, just to familiarize yourself with computer talk.

ACCESS MEMORY: To remove a word from memory and store it temporarily in a CPU register.

ACCESS TIME: The time that elapses between a call for data from a storage device and the availability of that data.

ACCUMULATOR: One of several registers which temporarily store, or "accumulate" the results of various operations.

ADAPTER: Any device through which two or more units, not otherwise compatible, can be made to operate together. See *interface*.

ADDER: An electronic circuit that adds two numbers together.

ADDRESS: The designation of a specific location in memory or of an I/O device.

ADDRESS BUS: A line along which the address is transmitted from the central processing unit to memory and I/O peripherals.

ADDRESS REGISTER: A register used for storing an address.

ADD TIME: The length of time it takes for a microprocesser to add two numbers of several digits. The relative speed of a microprocessor is often given in terms of add time.

ALGORITHM: A sequence of operations, either mathematical or logical, or both, which, when followed, achieve a predictable result such as a solution to a problem, an operation, or the establishment of a set of circumstances.

ALPHANUMERICS: The Roman alphabet in upper and lower case and the digits 0 through 9.

ALU: Abbreviation for arithmetic/logic unit.

ANSI: American National Standards Institute, an organization dedicated to the establishment of industrial standards, including standards for computers.

APPLICATION SOFTWARE: See *software*.

ARCHITECTURE: Literally, the structure of a computer system. The term involves the physical hardware, the manner and order in which processing is performed, the arrangement of the elements of a computer, even the circuitry on the chips. The bus, storage, and control capacities of a microcomputer are all parts of its architecture.

ARITHMETIC/LOGIC UNIT (ALU): That portion of a central processing unit where the mathematical and logical operations are carried out.

ASCII: Acronym for *American Standard Code* for *Information Interchange*. This code, widely used by microcomputers for the transmission of data between a central processing unit and its I/O peripherals, consists of 128 letters, numbers, punctuation marks, and special symbols each of which consists of a binary pattern that uses seven binary digits. The remaining bit, called a parity bit, is used to detect certain errors.

ASSEMBLER: A software program which converts symbolic or mnemonic language into machine language.

ASSEMBLY LANGUAGE: A programming language that uses mnemonics to show what each instruction does when it is carried out. Assembly language requires more knowledge and skill than so-called high-level language, but is easier to use than machine language.

ASYNCHRONOUS: When the data signals between two or more units of equipment are not timed by the frequency of a common clock, they are said to be asynchronous. When such an asynchronous state exists, it is handled by a process known as handshaking (which see).

BASIC: Acronym for *Beginner's All-purpose Symbolic Instruction Code*—a high-level programming language that is particularly popular among users of microcomputers because of its relative simplicity for programming.

BATCH PROCESSING: The processing of data that has been input at some time prior to the time that the actual processing is being performed. See *real time*.

BAUD: A unit by which signal speeds are measured. In microprocessing, the baud rate refers to the number of bits per second.

BCD: Abbreviation for Binary Coded Decimal.

BCD-TO-DECIMAL CONVERTER: An inexpensive integrated circuit chip which changes BCD to the decimal system. (Sometimes called a decoder.)

BENCHMARK: A test program or test problem which is used to make comparisons between computers. Criteria may be speed, memory requirements, costs, ease of programming, etc.

BINARY: A number system that has 2 as its base, and that uses only the digits 0 and 1. The binary numbering system is used by digital computers to perform the various tasks that are involved in data processing.

BINARY CODED DECIMAL (BCD): A system in which a binary code is used to represent a decimal number.

BINARY-TO-BCD CONVERSION: The conversion of a binary number into its equivalent in BCD.

BINARY-TO-DECIMAL CONVERSION: The conversion of a binary number into its equivalent decimal number.

BINARY-TO-HEXADECIMAL CONVERSION: The conversion of a binary number into its equivalent number in the hexadecimal (i.e. base-16) system.

BINARY-TO-OCTAL CONVERSION: The conversion of a binary number to its equivalent in the octal (i.e. base-8) number system.

BIT: Contraction of *bi*nary dig*it*.

BIT RATE: The number of bits transmitted per second.

BITS PER INCH (BPI): A measurement of the number of positions per linear inch of some recording media—such as magnetic tape—which can contain one bit of information.

BLOCK DIAGRAM: A fairly simple drawing showing the layout of a computer system. The major components are indicated by rectangles which are connected by straight lines. A typical block diagram for a microcomputer will include the CPU, ROM, RAM, the I/O interface, and the clock. Arrows are drawn to show the direction of the flow of data. The purchaser of a complete computer system will find a block diagram useful in visualizing the basic contents of the box and their various functions. Someone who wants to develop his own system will almost certainly need to begin with a block diagram.

BOOLEAN LOGIC: Mathematical logic processes based on a system of algebra developed in the early nineteenth century by English mathematician George Boole. Boolean logic plays a significant part in the various functions and operations performed by a computer.

BOOTSTRAP: A term used to describe either a device or a technique which brings itself into a desired state by means of an action which it performs itself. For example, a bootstrap loader is a short program for the first few steps of a program designed to load the rest of the program into the computer.

BPI: Abbreviation for bits per inch.

BPS: Abbreviation for bits per second.

BRANCH INSTRUCTION: A programming instruction that causes the computer to discontinue the sequential program instructions and move to another location in memory. The major types of branch instructions are "branch-on-condition" and "branch-unconditional." The branch-on-condition instruction tells the computer to perform a branch when some specified condition occurs. The branch-unconditional instruction always requires a transfer to another part of the program when this instruction is reached.

BREADBOARD: In the jargon of microcomputers, a breadboard is a fixture on which electronic circuitry that is being worked on is mounted. "To breadboard" is to spread out the circuitry so as to facilitate its assembly and testing.

BUG: A defect or an error, either in the hardware or the software, which causes the system to malfunction. See *debug*.

BULK STORAGE: Memory units in which large amounts of data may be stored. This data is transferred to the bulk storage equipment from the main memory of a computer and may be recalled later as needed.

BUS: A conductor or a set of conductors in parallel used to transmit data, signals, or power between parts of a computer system.

BUS DRIVER: An electronic amplifier designed to provide sufficient power to either control or activate electronic circuits that are connected to a great many devices. (Sometimes called line driver.)

BUS SYSTEM: All of the buses in a computer system that connect the computer to its peripherals.

BYTE: Eight bits. Most microcomputers use data words of eight bits, so in microprocessing, byte is generally synonymous with "word."

CAGE: A chassis used for mounting printed circuit cards. (Also known as "card cage.")

CARD: A board with a printed circuit; also a punched card (which see).

CARD EXTENDER: A device which enables a card to be removed from its chassis for testing. The card is plugged into the extender and the extender is then plugged into the space previously occupied by the card. This raises the card above the other cards and permits examination and testing.

CARD PUNCH: A device which records information by punching holes in cards. The holes represent letters, digits, and special characters.

CARD READER: A device that senses the holes in punched cards and translates them into machine code.

CATHODE RAY TUBE (CRT): An electronic vacuum tube, such as a television picture tube, that can be used to display graphic images. CRT terminals are popular I/O devices for microcomputers.

CELL: A memory location which may be capable of storing only one bit, but usually refers to a register capable of storing a word or instruction.

CENTRAL PROCESSING UNIT (CPU): A unit of a computer that handles the decoding and execution of instructions, controls the use of memory, performs arithmetic functions, etc. The CPU, which usually consists of an arithmetic/logic unit (ALU), several special temporary registers, and control circuitry, is the heart of a computer system.

CHARACTER: Anything that is used to represent, organize, and transmit data; it may be a letter of the alphabet, a digit, a punctuation mark, or any special symbol (such as the plus sign or equal sign).

CHIP: A very small silicon wafer containing an integrated circuit.

CLOCK: A device which generates electronic pulses by which all of the components of a computer system are synchronized. "Clock" also refers to the series of pulses themselves.

CLOCK PULSE (CP): The synchronization signal which is the time unit within a computer system.

CODE: A set of unique symbols used to represent data or information, and the rules setting forth the way in which those symbols can be used.

CODER: An electronic circuit which encodes.

COMPILER: A program which converts a program written in a high-level language into machine language.

CONDITIONAL JUMP: Branch-on-condition. See *branch instruction*.

CONSOLE: The control panel of the computer that permits the operator to use the system.

CONTROL BLOCK: The electronic circuitry in the central processing unit that performs the control function; also, a storage area used by a program to hold control information.

CONTROLLER: An adapter which permits the control of an I/O device by the central processing unit.

CONVERTER: Electronic circuitry, or a device, that converts data from one code into another code.

CORE MEMORY: A main storage device comprised of tiny magnetic cores looped around the intersections in a grid of fine wires. Not many microcomputers—if any—use core memory, but a great many larger systems do.

CP: Abbreviation for clock pulse.

CPU: Abbreviation for central processing unit.

CROM: Acronym for *Control Read-Only Memory*, a part of most CPU chips. The CROM is the storage area for detailed instructions assembled by the CPU to enable the performance of more complex instructions such as addition, subtraction, etc.

CRT: Abbreviation for cathode ray tube.

DATA: Basically data is information. It must be arranged first in a manner that enables it to be communicated to a computer, and second, in a form that the computer can operate on, or "process." Everything that goes into a computer may be classified as data, but generally, the term "instructions" refers to those words that tell the computer what to do, and "data" refers to the information that is to be processed.

DATA BASE: The total quantity of data that is available to a computer for making calculations and decisions. IBM defines data base as "a collection of data fundamental to an enterprise."

DATA BUS: See *bus*.

DATA POINTER: A CPU register that temporarily holds the address of the next byte that is to be brought from memory.

DATA PROCESSING: The performance of a systematic sequence of operations—mathematical, logical, or both—which a computer performs on data.

DATA RETRIEVAL: The bringing of data from storage—typically, bulk storage—to a location where it can be used or processed.

DEBUG: To seek out the source of errors or malfunctions, in computer hardware or in a program, that prevent the efficient or normal operation of the program or the computer system. It is also the name of a program sometimes used for trouble-shooting. See *bug*.

DECIMAL-TO-BCD CONVERSION: The conversion of a decimal number to its equivalent Binary-Coded-Decimal number.

DECIMAL-TO-BINARY CONVERSION: The conversion of a decimal number to its equivalent binary (base-2) number.

DECIMAL-TO-HEXADECIMAL CONVERSION: The conversion of decimal number to its equivalent hexadecimal (base-16) number.

DECIMAL-TO-OCTAL CONVERSION: The conversion of a decimal number to its equivalent octal (base-8) number.

DECODE: To translate from one code to another; also, to translate data back into the language in which it was originally written.

DECODER: A device or system used to decode.

DEDICATION: The assignment of a program, an I/O device, or an entire system to a single application or purpose.

DISK: A plate resembling a phonograph record and coated with magnetic material on which data may be "recorded" in great quanti-

ties for subsequent retrieval. "Floppy" disks are flexible and somewhat less costly to use. There are floppy-disk storage units which are compatible with microcomputers. These tend to be somewhat expensive and are best suited for business applications.

DISKETTE: A "floppy" disk. See *disk*.

DOCUMENTATION: All of the written material that is necessary to establish and operate a computer system. This includes (but is not necessarily limited to) the instruction manual, maintenance information, program descriptions, etc.

DOWN: When a computer system or one of its components is unable to function because of a programming error, a power failure, or a repair or maintenance problem, the system or component is said to be "down." Compare *up and running*.

DUMP: A print-out of the contents of a section of memory. "To dump" is to render such a print-out.

DYNAMIC STORAGE: A highly volatile memory which requires recharging at regular intervals to prevent the loss of data. See *volatility*.

EAROM: An abbreviation for Electrically Alterable Read-Only Memory, a ROM whose automatic erasure can be programmed. See *PROM* and *ROM*.

EBCDIC: Abbreviation for Extended Binary Coded Decimal Interchange, a character code widely used by computers.

EDIT: To change portions of a computer program or data by making insertions, deletions, or corrections.

EDITOR: A program or a portion of a program designed for a specific computer to be used for editing. The editor simplifies insertions and deletions by automatically renumbering the instructions and then producing a new program listing with the revisions.

EDP: Abbreviation for electronic data processing.

EPROM: Abbreviation for Erasable Programmable Read-Only Memory. Like other

PROMs, an EPROM can be electrically programmed. However, using an ultraviolet light, that program can be erased and another program entered.

EXECUTIVE PROGRAM: A program that controls or supervises the execution of other programs or the overall operation of a system.

EXPANSION CARD: A card on which chips or circuits can be mounted. The card is then added to the system to expand its capability.

FIRMWARE: A program that has been implanted in a read-only memory (ROM) device.

FLAG: In microcomputers, register that indicates the existence of a particular condition in the computer system.

FLIP-FLOP: An electronic circuit of two opposite polarities, the interchange of which is controlled by a signal from the clock. A number of elements of a microcomputer use flip-flops, including flag registers.

FLOPPY DISK: See *disk*.

FLOPPY-DISK DRIVE: A device which permits the CPU to write to or read from a floppy disk. (Sometimes called a "loader.")

FLOWCHART: A diagram showing the "flow" or sequential steps of a computer program.

HALF-ADDER: One of the components of a full adder.

HANDSHAKING: Signals or pulses that establish synchronization between an asynchronous I/O unit and the computer.

HARD COPY: A computer's output that is printed on paper.

HARDWARE: The physical components of a computer system—the electronics, the wires, the plastic, the glass, and the metal. (Compare firmware, software.)

HEX: Hexadecimal.

HEXADECIMAL NUMBER SYSTEM: A number system that uses 16 as its base. A hexadecimal code is used as a shorthand method of writing lengthy binary words or numbers. Because hexadecimal is especially useful when words are divisible by 4, it is a popular code for microcomputer programmers.

HIGH-LEVEL LANGUAGE: A computer programming language that is easier and more convenient for the programmer. The computer can convert the high-level language to machine language. BASIC is the most common high-level language used with microcomputers.

HITS: Acronym for *Hobbyist's Interchange Tape Standard*, a data recording format that utilizes tape cassettes and is designed to permit an interchange of cassettes and programs among some hobbyists.

IC: Abbreviation for integrated circuits.

INFORMATION RETRIEVAL: See *data retrieval*.

INPUT: A signal emanating from a peripheral device and going into the central processing unit. Also, "to input" is to place data into the data processing system. Also, the data itself.

INPUT/OUTPUT (I/O) DEVICE: Any peripheral hardware which is used to input data to the computer or take data (output) from the computer. I/O devices may be CRT terminals, printers, various storage devices, etc.

INPUT PORT: See *I/O port*.

INTEGRATED CIRCUIT (IC): A complete electronic circuit contained on a minute chip of silicon. Integrated circuits may consist of only a few transistors, resistors, diodes, capacitors, etc., or thousands of them. They are generally classified, according to the complexity of the circuitry, as Small-Scale Integration (SSI), Medium-Scale Integration (MSI), Large-Scale Integration (LSI), and Very-Large-Scale Integration (VLSI).

INTERFACE: The place or boundary line where two pieces of equipment or hardware meet. An interface is also a piece of hardware—an adapter—which makes two pieces of equipment compatible. "Interface" is sometimes used as a verb.

INTERNAL MEMORY: A computer's main, high-speed memory, that is contained within the computer, as opposed to peripheral bulk storage.

INTERPRETER: A compiler program that converts one instruction at a time into machine language.

INTERRUPT: A signal from an I/O device to the central processing unit requesting some form of action. Through a series of procedures, the CPU interrupts the program it is following and attends to the task called for by the interrupt signal. The CPU then returns to the execution of its program.

I/O: Abbreviation for input/output.

I/O Device: See *input/output device*.

I/O PORT: A port designed for use in conjunction with an I/O device. See *port*.

JUMP: See *branch*.

K: Abbreviation for the prefix kilo- (of Greek origin), meaning one thousand. A kilometer is a thousand meters. Computer memory is given in terms of thousands of bytes or kilobytes; 8,000 bytes=8 Kilobytes=8K.

KEYBOARD: The typewriter-like portion of an I/O device, such as a CRT terminal or a Teletypewriter. Also often used to designate the numerical keyboard of a calculator, although this is more commonly referred to as a keypad.

KEYPAD: See *keyboard*.

KILOBAUD: A thousand bauds.

KILOBIT: A thousand bits.

KILOBYTE: A thousand bytes.

LABEL: An alphabetical, numerical, or symbolic means of identifying specific memory addresses or locations in a program.

LANGUAGE: Any system of communication of ideas and information that uses a set of fixed symbols in accordance with specific rules. Computer languages permit communication between people and computers.

LARGE-SCALE INTEGRATION (LSI): See *integrated circuit*.

LED: Abbreviation for light-emitting diode, a semiconductor electronic device which, as part of an I/O device, displays letters or numbers in a read-out; usually red or green.

LIGHT PEN: An input device resembling a pen and containing a photocell and photomultiplier. It is used for "writing" on a CRT.

LINE DRIVER: Synonymous with bus driver.

LIQUID CRYSTAL DISPLAY (LCD): A type of read-out used in I/O devices; many digital watches and quite a few hand-held calculators now use LCDs in preference to LEDs.

LOAD: To enter data into a computer's memory or registers.

LOADER: A computer program that takes another program from storage and loads it into the computer.

LOCATION: The memory cell in which a data word or instruction is stored.

LOGIC CIRCUITRY: The hardware that performs logical operations.

LOGICAL EXPRESSION: A logical relationship expressed in Boolean algebra.

LOOP: A set of computer instructions carried out repeatedly until some condition occurs that instructs the computer to discontinue the looping process.

LSI: Abbreviation for large-scale integration. See *integrated circuit*.

MACHINE CODE: Synonymous with machine language (which see).

MACHINE LANGUAGE: A language consisting of a binary code. Computers "understand" only machine language, so all other programming languages must be converted to machine language prior to being entered into the CPU.

MAGNETIC CORE: See *core*.

MAGNETIC TAPE: Basically, recording tape of the type used in tape recorders. For expensive, large computers, the magnetic oxide material with which the plastic tape is coated may differ somewhat to conform to the specific purpose for which the tape is to be used. Among microcomputer users, however, the tape cassette has become a popular means of bulk storage, and the inexpensive variety available almost anywhere has proven both economical and useful. Magnetic tape is sometimes called "mag" tape.

MAINFRAME: Three different sources offer three different definitions of "main frame." One source claims that the word refers to the computer itself—i.e. the CPU and memory—and specifically excludes peripherals. Another source claims that mainframe is synonymous with central processing unit. A third source claims that the mainframe is the computer chassis holding the printed circuit cards. They are all more or less correct, depending on context.

MAINFRAME SLOT: A slot in the chassis of a microcomputer in which PC cards are placed. Many microcomputers have empty slots which allow for subsequent expansion of the system.

MASS STORAGE DEVICE: A kind of electronic file cabinct which retains large quantities of data from a computer's memory for possible later retrieval.

MEDIUM-SCALE INTEGRATION (MSI): *See integrated circuit.*

MEGA-: A prefix (from the Greek) meaning one million. A megabyte is a million bytes.

MEMORY: The facility in a computer where data is entered and stored for use in the immediate or long-term future. "Memory" and "storage" are often used interchangeably.

MEMORY ALLOCATION: The designation of memory cells for a specific purpose.

MEMORY PROTECT: A means of protecting against the loss of data from memory. Memory protection may be hardware, firmware, or software. Memory can be lost through power failure, through variations in current or voltage, or by accidentally "overwriting." This is comparable to recording over a magnetic tape and, in so doing, erasing the data previously recorded on that tape.

METAL OXIDE SEMICONDUCTOR (MOS): A type of transistor technology widely used in microcomputer systems.

MICRO-: A prefix (from the Greek) that means "small" or one millionth, depending on context. It is often signified by the Greek letter *mu,* which looks like this: μ. Because of the absence of this symbol in most typewriters and type fonts, "micro" is frequently and erroneously represented by a lower case "u."

MICROCOMPUTER: A small computer whose CPU is an integrated circuit embedded in a semiconductor chip. Integrated circuit technology has made it possible to develop small computers with enormous capabilities.

MICROPROCESSOR: A central processing unit that is comprised of one or several semiconductor chips.

MICROSECOND: A millionth of a second; abbreviated μsec or usec.

MILLISECOND: A thousandth of a second; abbreviated ms.

MINICOMPUTER: A computer that is larger than a microcomputer but smaller than a big computer. (For some reason, one never hears the term "maxicomputer.") Whether a computer is a mini or a micro depends somewhat on price and memory size. There are, however, no clear-cut distinctions between the two categories.

MODEM: Acronym for *mo*dulator/*de*modulator, a device that converts data so that it can be transmitted over communications (e.g. telephone) lines, and reconverts the data at the receiving end.

MOS: See *metal oxide semiconductor.*

MOTHERBOARD: An assembly board on which printed circuits can be interconnected through a bus.

MPU: Abbreviation for microprocessor

unit or microprocessing unit; synonymous with *CPU* (which see).

MSI: Abbreviation for medium-scale integration. See *integrated circuit*.

NANOSECOND: A billionth of a second.

NIBBLE: Half a byte; a word consisting of four bits. Sometimes spelled "nybble."

NUMBER-CRUNCHING: Descriptive of a computer or a program whose purpose is to perform large quantities of arithmetical computations.

NYBBLE: See *nibble*.

OBJECT PROGRAM: A program that has been translated into a form readable by the computer. Compare *source program*.

OCTAL: A numbering system with a base of 8.

OCTAL-TO-BINARY CONVERSION: The conversion of an octal (base-8) number to its equivalent binary (base-2) number.

OCTAL-TO-DECIMAL CONVERSION: The conversion of an octal (base-8) number to its decimal (base-10) equivalent.

ONLINE: A peripheral unit operating in conjunction with a computer is said to be online.

OUTPUT: The data which a computer transmits to a peripheral device. Also used as a verb: "to output."

PAPER TAPE: See *punched tape*.

PARALLEL-TO-SERIES CONVERTER: Circuitry which takes data being fed in parallel (i.e. along several pathways simultaneously) and converts it to serial transmission (i.e. over a single pathway). Compare *series-to-parallel converter*.

PARALLEL TRANSMISSION: The transmission of data along several pathways at the same time. Compare *serial transmission*.

PARITY: The odd or even number of 1's in a binary word, byte, character, or message. The importance of parity is in its use as a code for detecting errors.

PC CARD or BOARD: See *printed circuit card*.

PERFORATED TAPE: See *punched tape*.

PERIPHERAL: Descriptive of devices that work in conjunction with, but are not part of, the computer, such as CRT terminals, Teletypewriters, printers, tape recorders, etc. Often the word is used as a noun and one speaks of such a device as a "peripheral."

PIN: A connection terminal of an integrated circuit.

PORT: A terminal through which data goes into or comes out of a computer.

PRINTED CIRCUIT (PC) CARD: A card made of plastic material onto which electronic components and circuitry are mounted. Sometimes called a "PC board."

PRINTER: Any one of several peripherals delivering hard-copy print-outs of computerized data.

PRINT-OUT: The output of a printer. Also used as a verb: "to print out."

PROCESSOR: A program which provides for compilation, translation, and various other functions of a specific programming language. Also, a "processor" is anything which does processing.

PROGRAM: For computers, a program is a set of sequential instructions designed to achieve a specific result, and which a computer is capable of accepting. Also, "to program" is to write such a set of instructions.

PROGRAMMER: A person who designs, writes, and tests programs. (However, these separate functions are sometimes performed by different people.)

PROM: Acronym for *Programmable Read-Only Memory*, a read-only memory that the user of a microcomputer can program himself, using a device known as a PROM burner. PROMs that can be erased and reprogrammed are known as EROMs (Erasable Read-Only Memories) or EPROMs (Erasable Programmable Read-Only Memories). See *ROM*.

PROM BURNER: A device which "etches" programs into PROMs; also called a PROM programmer.

PULSE: An electrical signal of rapidly alternating voltage levels, used to transmit data.

PUNCHED CARD: A card on which holes have been punched to represent letters, digits, and special characters. The holes are sensed by a card reader which translates the data represented by the holes into machine code.

PUNCHED TAPE: A mylar or paper strip approximately an inch wide, onto which data is encoded by means of a series of holes punched into the tape.

RAM: Abbreviation for Random-Access Memory.

RANDOM-ACCESS MEMORY (RAM): A computer memory that has been arranged into cells, any one of which can be "accessed" directly, rather than having to go through cells sequentially to reach the one that is desired. In a microcomputer, RAM refers to read/write memory that serves as a scratch pad, a temporary place to hold data, partial results, program instructions, etc.

READ-OUT: A display on an LED, LCD, CRT or other visual device.

REAL TIME: A term that describes the processing of data as soon as it is received. Compare *batch processing*.

REGISTER: A temporary memory location in a microcomputer.

RETRIEVAL: See *data retrieval*.

ROM: Acronym for *Read-Only Memory*. Computer memory which can be read, but cannot be written to. The pattern of a ROM is fixed and unalterable and is therefore useful for fixed data, program instructions, etc. Compare *EPROM,* and *PROM*.

ROUTINE: A set of instructions to be carried out in sequence by the computer for the purpose of achieving a specific function. A routine is a kind of program within a program. (It is sometimes called a "subroutine.")

SCRATCH-PAD MEMORY: See *RAM*.

SEMICONDUCTOR: An element, usually silicon or germanium, which, when diffused with certain impurities, becomes a carrier of positive or negative electrical charges. Semiconductor technology has made possible the manufacture of minuscule electrical circuits, giving rise to microprocessors and several important new industries.

SERIAL TRANSMISSION: The transmission of data over a single pathway. Compare *parallel transmission*.

SERIES-TO-PARALLEL CONVERTER: A register which accepts data in series and outputs that data in parallel. Compare *parallel-to-series converter*.

SMALL-SCALE INTEGRATION (SSI): See *integrated circuit*.

SOFTWARE: A computer's programs. System software includes programs that enable the system to function, such as compilers, assemblers, interpreters, executive programs, etc. Application software usually refers to programs intended to solve problems or produce results. Also, many microcomputer users consider software to be anything that does not qualify as hardware or firmware.

SOURCE LANGUAGE: The language in which a program is written. If the source language is high level, then it will be translated into object language.

SOURCE PROGRAM: A program that has been written in source language and which will be converted to an object program.

SSI: Abbreviation for small-scale integration. See *integrated circuit*.

STORAGE: See *memory*.

SUBROUTINE: A portion of a program or a routine that may be used repeatedly during a program. See *routine*.

SYMBOLIC LANGUAGE: A programming language that uses a mnemonic code.

SYSTEM: A group of elements that interact to form an entity. A computer system minimally consists of a central processing unit, an input device, and an output device. Other components may be added to the system as need requires.

SYSTEMS ANALYST: A person who analyzes a system in order to make improvements or solve problems.

TAPE: Punched tape or magnetic tape.

TAPE CASSETTE: A cassette containing magnetic recording tape. It is one of the most economical and, therefore, one of the most popular bulk storage media for microcomputers.

TAPE PUNCH: A device which makes the holes in punched tape.

TAPE READER: A device which reads the holes in punched tape and enters the data into the computer.

TEMPLATE: A plastic stencil for flowchart symbols.

TEXT EDITOR: See *editor*.

THROUGHPUT RATE: The speed with which a computer processes data and produces a result.

TIME SHARING: A term that describes the simultaneous use of a central processing unit by two or more users, often remote from the CPU and each other. Actually, the simultaneity is an illusion. The CPU is handling each I/O sequentially, but with such incredible speed that delays are barely perceptible (except when heavy demands are made on a large computer).

TTY: Abbreviation for Teletypewriter, a registered trademark of the Teletype Corporation.

u: A substitute for the symbol μ, the Greek letter *mu*, which stands for micro-.

uC: Abbreviation for microcomputer.

uP: Abbreviation for microprocessor.

UP AND RUNNING: When a computer or one of its components has been "down" and is restored to full operation, it is said to be "up and running."

VERY-LARGE-SCALE INTEGRATION (VLSI): See *integrated circuit*.

VIDEO: In microcomputers, descriptive of any terminal which uses a CRT screen, such as a television set.

VLSI: Very-large-scale integration. See *integrated circuit*.

VOLATILITY: The condition of memories and registers that lose their data when power is turned off or interrupted. Also, certain memories and registers which must be continually refreshed by the power supply to prevent the loss of data are said to be volatile.

WORD: A group of characters that the computer treats as a single unit.

WORD LENGTH: The number of bits that make up a word. Most microcomputers use 8-bit words; therefore byte and word are used interchangeably.

WRITE: To enter data into memory or a register or onto an output medium such as tape or paper.

APPENDIX I
BIBLIOGRAPHY

• Books

It is difficult to recommend supplementary reading. You have already finished reading a book intended to introduce you to the area of home computers. From this point, it becomes a question of your own technological expertise. Probably the best course to follow is to wait until you have a computer of your very own, thoroughly study the instruction manual that comes with it, and then shop around the book department of a computer store for the book or books that you feel are best suited to bring you to the next level of advancement. In the absence of a convenient computer store, you could take a chance and order some books by mail. You will find many advertisements for books in computer magazines (about which more shortly). And if that does not appeal to you, then perhaps you can try getting started with any of the books that follow.

For a general introduction to the world of the computer, although without much reference to microcomputers, there are two excellent works. One is *Computers Made Really Simple* by Kent Porter, published by Thomas Y. Crowell Company. The other is *How You Can Learn to Live with Computers* by Harry Kleinberg, published by J. B. Lippincott Com-

pany. These books should be available at the public library; if they are not, your book dealer can easily order them from the publishers.

The other books mentioned here are less likely to appear in the average book shop or book department of a department store. You will find them in computer stores, or they can be ordered from the publisher or from one of the mail-order firms specializing in books on computing. Such firms advertise in the various computer magazines.

A Dictionary of Microcomputing by Philip E. Burton is an absolute must. With only a few exceptions, the hundreds of definitions in this book are clear, concise, and readily understandable. It is published by Garland Publishing, Inc., 545 Madison Avenue, New York, New York 10022.

Adam Osborne is the author or co-author of several useful books on microcomputers which he markets through his own company. *An Introduction to Microcomputers: Volume 0, the Beginner's Book,* has much of the information that the book you are now holding contains, but it is more technically oriented. It takes the beginner who has no knowledge of or background in computers literally inside the machine with many photographs and diagrams. It is a good way to obtain a painless and gentle introduction to the technical aspects of a personal computer. *An Introduction to Microcomputers: Volume 1, Basic Concepts,* picks up where Volume 0 leaves off. (The numbering system would suggest that Volume 0 was published as an afterthought.) Both volumes can be purchased from Osborne and Associates, Inc., P.O Box 2036, Berkeley, California 94702.

To teach yourself BASIC, try *Beginning BASIC* by Paul Chirlian, available from Dilithium Press, Forest Grove, Oregon 97116. Another BASIC book is *INSTANT BASIC* by Gerald Brown, published by Dymax, P.O. Box 310, Menlo Park, California 94025.

If you like the idea of playing games with your computer, you might try *What to Do After You Hit Return,* published by People's Computer Company, Menlo Park, California 94025, and *101 Basic Computer Games,* by David H. Ahl, published by Creative Computing, Morristown, New Jersey 07960.

If you have a video display terminal that you'd like to get to know better, or want to design or modify one, try the *TV Typewriter Cookbook* by Don Lancaster, published by Howard W. Sams and Company, Inc., Indianapolis, Indiana 46268. This book will also show you how to modify an IBM Selectric typewriter for use as a peripheral.

In addition to the books described here, the publishers whose addresses are given above have long lists of other books designed for the owner of a microcomputer. For example, Osborne has a number of books on programming, including accounting software in BASIC. Do not hesitate to write to any of these publishers for a complete list of currently available books.

● **Periodicals**

Magazines and journals on microprocessing have proliferated almost as fast as the industry itself. My personal favorite is *ROM,* which astute readers will recognize as the acronym for read-only memory, certainly an appropriate name for a microprocessing magazine. There seems to be a tendency, particularly among computer hobbyists, toward excessive cuteness, coupled with a certain free-wheeling attitude that seems to have particular appeal for a type of individual I can only describe as a technological hippy—the sort of person who says, "Yes, technology is fine and computer technology is really super, but we've got to get it out of the hands of the establishment, who are, of course, screwing it up." Happily, *ROM* is devoid of both excessive cuteness and pseudo-political posturing. This magazine is professional in every way and contains articles that are timely, interesting, and understandable even to the novice. If there is a magazine dealer near you who carries a wide variety of titles, he may be able to supply you with a copy of *ROM;* otherwise, pick it up at your computer store, or write to ROM Publications Inc., Route 97, Hampton, Connecticut 06247 for subscription rates. They may even be willing to send you a single sample copy. (This holds true, by the way, for all the periodicals listed here: a newsdealer is not likely to have them, but a computer store most certainly will, and all of them can be ordered by subscription from the publisher.)

The publications which follow are all, in my opinion, of fairly high quality. Physical style and editorial concept differ and preference of one over another is essentially a matter of personal taste. At the risk of repetition, I must point out that they can all be seen at a computer store, along with perhaps a dozen or more publications dedicated to personal computing.

BYTE is probably the largest of the microcomputing publications, at least at present. It calls itself "the small systems journal." It is published by BYTE Publications, 70 Main Street, Peterborough, New Hampshire 03458.

Kilobaud is jammed with information about hardware and software and appears to be one of the favorites among hobbyists. It is published by *Kilobaud,* Peterborough, New Hampshire 03458.

Interface Age Magazine advertises that its articles range from the fundamentals of computers to languages and systems design. Applications include both professional and nontechnical. Available from *Interface Age Magazine,* P.O. Box 1234, Cerritos, California 90701.

Creative Computing features noncommercial applications of computers. Articles cover the application of computers to educational uses, visual arts, games, music, etc. Write to *Creative Computing,* P.O. Box 789, Morristown, New Jersey 07960.

Personal Computing tends to be somewhat more general in its scope and includes material for people who not only enjoy working with computers but like to read about them as well. It is available from Benwill Publishing Corporation, Box 335, Winchester, Massachusetts 01890.

APPENDIX II
COMPUTER SOCIETIES

I shall have to begin this section with a disclaimer: Most of the addresses given below are those of club presidents, secretaries, or other club officers. As in any social group, those positions change frequently and rapidly. This list is about as accurate as possible at the time of writing.

Before you even consider contacting any of these clubs, you should decide whether a computer club is for you. If you are interested in learning more about personal computing, the answer is an unequivocal yes. If you are really enjoying your personal computer, if in addition to performing practical tasks it is a source of pleasure and diversion for you, a computer club can probably help make it more so. Of course, there are bound to be some small, cliquish groups that will not welcome newcomers, but they tend to be very much the exception rather than the rule.

Even if you are not the club-joining type, it may be worth your while to at least establish contact with a computer society to gain the answers to some questions you have about microcomputers in general or one microcomputer in particular.

● **Alabama**

North Alabama Computer Club
c/o Jack Crenshaw
1409 Blevins Gap Road, S.E.
Huntsville 35802

● **California**

Bay Area Microprocessor Users Group
4565 Black Avenue
Pleasanton 94506

Beverly Hills High School Computer Club
241 Marino Drive
Beverly Hills 90212

Computer Guild
P.O. Box 255232
Sacramento 95825

Computer Organization of Los Angeles
P.O. Box 43677
Los Angeles 90043

Computer Phreaques United
c/o Mac McCormick
2090 Cross Street
Seaside 93955

Glendale Community College Computer Club
c/o V. X. Lashieu
1500 North Verdugo Road
Glendale 92108

Homebrew Computer Club
P.O. Box 626
Mountain View 94042

Litton Calculator/Computer Club
Litton Guidance & Control Systems
MS 78/31
5500 Canoga Avenue
Woodland Hills 91364

LO*OP Center
8099 La Plaza
Cotati 94928

North Orange County Computer Club
P.O. Box 3603
Orange 92665

Sacramento Microcomputer Users Group
P.O. Box 161513
Sacramento 95816

San Diego Computer Society
P.O. Box 9988
San Diego 92109

San Gabriel SCCS
c/o Dan Erikson
400 South Catalina Avenue
Pasadena 91106

San Luis Obispo Microcomputer Club
439 B. Marsh Street
San Luis Obispo 93401

Santa Barbara Computer Group
c/o Glenn A. McComb
210 Barrunca, Apt. 2
Santa Barbara 93101

Santa Barbara Nameless Computer Club
c/o Doug Penrod
1445 La Clima Road
Santa Barbara 93101

6800 Computer Club
P.O. Box 18081
San Jose 95118

Southern California Computer Society
P.O. Box 987
South Pasadena 91030

Technical Developments
P.O. Box 2151
Oxnard 93034

29 Palms California Area Group
c/o Sgt. Wesley Isgrigg
74055 Casita Drive
Twenty-Nine Palms 92277

UCLA Computer Club
3514 Boelter Hall
UCLA
Los Angeles 90024

Valley Chapter, SCCS
c/o R. Stuart Gibbs
5652 Lemona Avenue
Van Nuys 91411

Ventura County Computer Society
P.O. Box 525
Port Hueneme 93041

● **Colorado**

Denver Amateur Computer Society
P.O. Box 6338
Denver 80206

● **Connecticut**

Amateur Computer Society
260 Noroton
Darien 06820

Connecticut Microists
c/o George Ahmuty
6011 Wendy Lane
Westport 06881

Connecticut SCCS
c/o Charles Floto
267 Willow Street
New Haven 06511

Fairchild F8 Users Club
c/o G. W. Hemphill
132 Scott Swamp Road
Farmington 06032

University of Hartford
Microcomputer Club
College of Engineering—Dana Hall
200 Bloomfield Avenue
West Hartford 06117

● **District of Columbia**

Washington Amateur Computer Society
Robert Jones
4201 Massachusetts Avenue
Apt. 168W
Washington 20016

● **Florida**

Jacksonville Computer Club
9951 Atlantic Boulevard
Suite 326
Jacksonville 32211

Miami Area Computer Club
c/o Terry Williamson
P.O. Box 430852 S
Miami 33143

Miami Computer Club
c/o John Lynn
13431 S.W. 79th Street
Miami 33183

Computer Society of Florida
P.O. Box 3284
Downtown Station
Tampa 33604

South Florida Computer Group
1155 N.W. 14th Street
Miami 33123

Southern Florida Computer Society
c/o Roberto Denis
11080 N.W. 39th Street
Coral Springs 33065

Space Coast Microcomputer Club
c/o Ray O. Lockwood
1825 Canal Ct.
Merritt Island 32952

Tallahassee Amateur Computer Society
c/o Larry Hughes
Rt. 14, Box 351–116
Tallahassee 32304

University of Florida
Amateur Computer Society
Electrical Engineering Department
Room 234, Larson Hall
Gainesville 32611

● **Georgia**

Atlanta Area Microcomputer Club
c/o James Dunion
421 Ridgecrest Road
Atlanta 30307

Atlanta Area Microcomputer
Hobbyist Group
P.O. Box 33140
Atlanta 30332

● **Hawaii**

Aloha Computer Club
c/o Robert Kennedy
1541 Dominus No. 1404
Honolulu 96822

● **Idaho**

CSPCC
c/c Mark Bentley
205 Foster, Apt. 2
Coeur d'Alene 83814

• Illinois

Chicago Area Computer Hobbyist's Exchange
P.O. Box 36
Vernon Hill 60061

Altair-Chicago
517 Talcott Road
Park Ridge 60068

Chicago Area Microcomputer Users Group
c/o Bill Precht
1102 South Edison
Lombard 60148

Ice-Nine, Inc.
P.O. Box 291
Western Springs 60558

• Indiana

Bloomington Association for the
Computer Sciences
c/o Remy M. Simpson
901 East 13th Street
Bloomington 47401

Hoosier Amateur Computer and
Kluge Society
c/o Ray Borill
111 South College Avenue
Bloomington 47401

Indiana Small Systems Group
54 Sherry Lane
Brownsburg 46112

Louisville Area Computers Club
115 Edgemont Drive
New Albany 47150

Purdue University Computer Hobbyist Club
Room 67, Electrical Engineering
Purdue University
West Lafayette 47907

• Iowa

Eastern Iowa Computer Club
c/o Mike Wimble
6026 Undersood Avenue, S.W.
Cedar Rapids 52404

• Kansas

Computer Network of Kansas City
c/o Earl Day
968 Kansas Avenue
Kansas City 66105

South Central Kansas Amateur
Computer Association
c/o Cris Borger
1504 North St. Clair
Wichita 67203

• Kentucky

Louisville Area Computer Club
c/o Steve Roberts (Cybertronics)
P.O. Box 18065
Louisville 40218

• Louisiana

New Orleans Computer Club
Emile Alline
1119 Pennsylvania Avenue
Slikell 70458

• Massachusetts

Alcove Computer Club
c/o John P. Vullo
21 Sunset Avenue
North Reading 01864

Greater Boston Computer Users Group
c/o Steven Hain
40 Wilshire Drive
Sharon 02067

New England Computer Society
P.O. Box 198
Bedford 01730

• Michigan

Ann Arbor Computing Club
c/o Roger Gregory
1485 Newport Road
Ann Arbor 48103

Computer Hobbyists Around Lansing
c/o Joyce and Marvin Church
4307 Mar Moor Drive
Lansing 48917

Detroit Area Club
c/o Dennis Siemit
45466 Cluster
Utica 48087

Detroit Area Users Group
c/o Dana Badertscher
18300 Ash
East Detroit 48021

Mid-Michigan Computer Group
c/o Tony Preston
15151 Ripple Drive
Linden 48451

• Minnesota

Bit Users Association
Resources Access Center
3010 Fourth Avenue South
Minneapolis 55408

Minnesota Computer Society
c/o Jean Rice
Box 35317
Minneapolis 55435

Southern Minnesota Amateur Computer Club
2212 North West 17th Avenue
Rochester 55901

Nashua Area Computer Club
c/o Dwayne Jeffries
181 Cypress Lane
Nashua 03060

New England Computer Club
c/o BYTE
70 Main Street
Peterborough 03458

• New Jersey

Amateur Computer Group of New Jersey
c/o Sol Libes
UCTI
1776 Raritan Road
Scotch Plains 07076

Holmdel Microprocessor Club
c/o Fred Horney
Rm. 3D317
Bell Telephone Labs
Holmdel 07733

New Jersey Computer Club
c/o Bruce C. Dalland
37 Brook Drive
Dover 07801

Northern New Jersey Amateur
    Computer Group
c/o Murray P. Dwight
593 New York Avenue
Lyndhurst 07071

• New Mexico

Albuquerque Area Computer Club
Gary Tack
P.O. Box 866
Corrales 87048

• New York

Buffalo Computer Club
c/o Chuck Fischer
355 South Creek Drive
Depew 14043

Ithaca Computer Club
c/o Steve Edelman
204 Dryden Road
Ithaca 14850

Long Island Computer Association
c/o Dave Metal
28 Splitrail Place
Commack 11725

New York Amateur Computer Club
106 Bedford Street
New York 10014

New York Micro Hobbyist Group
c/o Robert Schwartz
375 Riverside Drive, Apt. 1E
New York 10025

Stony Brook Home-Brew Computer Club
c/o Ludwig Braun
College of Engineering and Applied Sciences
State University of New York
Stony Brook 11794

Pacesetter Users Group
1457 Broadway, Room 305
New York 10016

Niagara Region Computer Group
c/o Chuck Fischer
355 South Creek Drive
Depew 14043

Rochester Area Microcomputer Society
P.O. Box D
Rochester 14609

Students Cybernetics Lab
16 Linwood Avenue
Buffalo 14209

Westchester Amateur Computer Society
c/o Harold Shair
41 Colby Avenue
Rye 10576

Westchester-Fairfield Amateur
Computer Society
R.R. 1, Box 198
Pound Ridge 10576

• North Carolina

Triangle Amateur Computer Club
P.O. Box 17523
Raleigh 27609

• Ohio

Amateur Computer Society of Columbus
c/o Walter Marvin
408 Thurber Drive West, #6
Columbus 43215

Cleveland Digital Group
c/o John Kabat, Jr.
1200 Seneca Boulevard, No. 407
Broadway Heights 44147

Dayton Microcomputer Association
c/o Doug Andrews
8668 Sturbridge Avenue
Cincinnati 45200

Compute, Evaluate, Trade
P.O. Box 104
Tipp City 45371

Midwest Alliance of Computer Clubs
c/o Gary Coleman
P.O. Box 83
Brecksville 44141

• Oklahoma

Central Oklahoma Amateur Computing
  Society
c/o Lee Lilly
P.O. Box 2213
Norman 73069

Oklahoma City Computer Club
c/o Bill Cowden
2412 S.W. 45th
Oklahoma City 73119

Tulsa Computer Society
P.O. Box 1133
Tulsa 74101

● Oregon

Portland Computer Club
c/o Bill Marsh
2814 N.W. 40th Street
Portland 97212

Portland Computer Society
1003 Garland Street, Apt. 4
Woodburn 97071

● Pennsylvania

Central Pennsylvania Computer Club
c/o Joseph Pallas
1979 Crooked Oak
Lancaster 17601

Philadelphia Area Computer Society
P.O. Box 1954
Philadelphia 19105

Pittsburgh Area Computer Club
c/o Ed Dehart
400 Smithfield Road
Pittsburgh 15222

St. Thomas District High School
    Computer Club
1025 Braddock Avenue
Braddock 15104

Wilkes College Computer Club
c/o Erick Jansen, Math Dept.
Wilkes College
Wilkes-Barre 18703

● Texas

Alamo Computer Enthusiasts
c/o John Stanton
7417 Jonquil
San Antonio 78233

Central Texas Computer Association
c/o Ray McCoy
508 Blueberry Hill
Austin 78745

El Paso Computer Group
c/o Jack O. Coats, Jr.
213 Argonaut, Apt. 27
El Paso 79912

Houston Amateur Microcomputer Club
6513 Jackwood
Houston 77074

NASA-JSC Computer Hobbyist Club
c/o Marlowe Cassetti
1011 Davenport
Seabrook 77586

Northside Computer Group
2318 Townbreeze
San Antonio 78238

Panhandle Computer Society
c/o Tex Everett
2923 South Spring
Amarillo 79103

Permian Basin Computer Group
c/o John Rabenaldt
Ector Country School District
P.O. Box 3912
Odessa 79760

Texas A & M University
Microcomputer Club
P.O. Box M-9
Aggieland Station 77844

Texas Computer Club
c/o L. G. Walker
Rt. 1, Box 272
Aledo 76008

The Computer Hobbyist Group
    of North Texas
c/o Bill Fuller
2377 Dalworth 157
Grand Prairie 75050

● Utah

Salt Lake City Computer Club
2925 Valley View Avenue
Holladay 84117

- **Virginia**

Alexandria Chapter, CMC
c/o Richard Rubinstein
7711 Elba Road
Alexandria 22306

Charlottesville Computer Hobbyist Club
P.O. Box 6132
Charlottesville 22906

Dyna-Micro Users Group
c/o Dr. Frank Settle, Jr.
Digital Directions
P.O. Box 1053
Lexington 24450

Peninsula Computer Hobbyist Club
c/o Larry Polis
2 Weber Lane
Hampton 23663

Reston Chapter, CMC
Andrew Convery
2315 Freetown Center, Apt. 110
Reston 22091

- **Washington**

Northwest Computer Club
Box 242
Renton 98055

- **Wisconsin**

Durant Club
c/o James S. White
901 South 12th Street
Watertown 53094

Wisconsin Area Tribe of
    Computer Hobbyists
c/o Don Stevens
P.O. Box 159
Sheboygan Falls 53085

- **Canada**

Amateur Microprocessor Club of
    Kitchener-Waterloo
c/o Ed Spike
Electrical Engineering
University of Waterloo
Waterloo, Ontario N2L 3G1

Canadian Computer Club
861 111th Street
Brandon, Manitoba R7A 4L1

Montreal Area Computer Society
P.O. Box 613
Stock Exchange Tower
Montreal, Quebec

Toronto Region of Computer Enthusiasts
c/o Harold G. Melanson
Box 545
Streetsville, Ontario L5M 2C1

APPENDIX III
DEALERS

This list of dealers, while extensive, is by no means complete. Retailers come and go, and in this new and burgeoning field, the birth rate seems to far exceed the mortality rate. If your community is not represented here, check around a little.

An asterisk (*) indicates mail-order facilities.

NOTE: Inclusion in this list does not constitute an endorsement, recommendation, or the assumption of any responsibility by the author or publisher. *Caveat emptor!*

● **Alabama**

Computer Center
433 Valley Avenue Plaza
Birmingham 35209

Computerland
1550 Montgomery Highway
Birmingham 35226

Computerland
3020 University Drive, N.W.
Huntsville

● **Arizona**

*Tri-Tek, Inc.
6522 North 43rd Avenue
Glendale 85301

Bits & Bytes Computer Shop
6819 C. North 21st Avenue
Phoenix 85015

Byte Shop
28 West Camelback Road
Phoenix 85013

Byte Shop
12654 North 28th Drive
Phoenix 85019

Byte Shop
813 North Scottsdale Road
Tempe 85281

Altair Computer Center
4941 East 29th Street
Tucson 85711

Ancrona Corporation
4518 East Broadway
Tucson 85711

Byte Shop
2612 East Broadway
Tucson 85716

● **Arkansas**

Westark Computer Systems Inc.
2803 Rogers Avenue
Fort Smith 72901

Computer Products Unlimited
2412 South Broadway
Little Rock 72204

● **California**

Applied Computer Technology
2465 Fourth Street
Berkeley 94610

Byte Shop
1514 University Avenue
Berkeley 94703

Computer Kits
1044 University Avenue
Berkeley 94710

Kentucky Fried Computers
2465 Fourth Street
Berkeley 94710

Kush 'n' Stuff
60 Dillon Avenue
Campbell 95008

Sunshine Computer Company
9 Palomino Lane
Carson 90745

Micro Byte
183 East Eighth
Chico 95926

Bits, Bytes & Pieces
6211 Quincewood Circle
Citrus Heights 95710

Byte Citrus Heights
6041 Greenback Lane
Citrus Heights 95610

Computer Center
1913 Harbor Boulevard
Costa Mesa 92627

Ancrona Corporation
11080 Jefferson Boulevard
Culver City 90230

Action Audio Electronics
285 Lake Merced Boulevard
Daly City 94015

Computerland
11074 San Pablo Avenue
El Cerrito 94530

DCI Computer Systems
4670 North El Capitan
Fresno 93711

Bits 'n' Bytes
679 South State College Boulevard
Fullerton 92631

Data Center
136 North Maryland Avenue
Glendale 91206

Rainbow Enterprises
10723 White Oak Avenue
Granada Hills 91344

Computerland
22634 Foothill Boulevard
Hayward 94542

Computerland
6840 La Cienega Boulevard
Inglewood 90302

*Advanced Computer Products
P.O. Box 17329
Irvine 92713

Byte Shop
16508 Hawthorne Boulevard
Lawndale 90260

*Jade Company
5351 West 144th Street
Lawndale 90260

Bargain Electronics Enterprises
2018 Lomita Boulevard
Lomita 90717

A-Vid Electronics Company
1655 East 28th Street
Long Beach 90806

Arrowhead Computer Company
11656 West Rico Boulevard
Los Angeles 90064

Opamp/Computer
1033 North Sycamore Avenue
Los Angeles 90038

Computerland
24001 Via Fabricante
Mission Vieja 92675

Byte Shop
1063 West El Camino
Real Mountain View 94040

Digital Deli
80 West El Camino Real
Mountain View 94040

Wyle Distribution Group
2288 Charleston Road
Mountain View 94043

*Bill Godbout Electronics
P.O. Box 2355
Oakland 94614

Computer Mart
625 West Katella
Orange 92667

Byte Shop
2227 El Camino Real
Palo Alto 94306

Mr. Calculator
255 Town and Country Village
Palo Alto 94303

Byte Shop
496 South Lake Avenue
Pasadena 91101

*Electronics Warehouse Inc.
1603 Aviation Boulevard
Redondo Beach 90278

Micro-Computer
Application Systems
2322 Capitol Avenue
Sacramento 95816

*James Electronics
1021-A Howard Avenue
San Carlos 94070

The Computer Center
8205 Ronson Road
San Diego 92111

Computerland
4233 Convoy Street
San Diego 92111

*Integrated Circuits Unlimited
7889 Clairemont Mesa Boulevard
San Diego 92111

Byte Shop
321 Pacific Avenue
San Francisco 94111

Computerland
121 Fremont Street
San Francisco 94105

Computer Store of San Francisco
1093 Mission
San Francisco 94103

Small Business Computer Company
400 Dewey Boulevard
San Francisco 94116

*Ximedia
1290 24th Avenue
San Francisco 94122

Sunnysounds
927 East Lás Tunas Drive
San Gabriel 91776

Byte, Inc.
1450 Koll Circle
San Jose 95112

Byte Shop
2626 Union Avenue
San Jose 95124

Computer Room
124H Blossom Hill Road
San Jose 95123

Computerland
1922 Republic Avenue
San Leandro 94577

Computer Shack, Inc.
14860 Wicks Boulevard
San Leandro 94551

Prokotronics
439 Marsh Street
San Luis Obispo 93401

Terminal West
2185 Mountain View
San Luis Obispo 93401

Byte Shop
1200 West Hillsdale Boulevard
San Mateo 94403

Computerland
42 42nd Avenue
San Mateo 94403

Byte Shop
509 Francisco Boulevard
San Rafael 94901

Ancrona Corporation
1300 D East Edinger Avenue
Santa Ana 92705

Byte Shop
3 West Mission Street
Santa Barbara 93101

Channel Radio & Electronics
18 East Ortega Street
Santa Barbara 93101

Polymorphic, Inc.
460 Ward Drive
Santa Barbara 93111

Byte Shop
3400 El Camino Real
Santa Clara 95009

*Quest Electronics
P.O. Box 4330N
Santa Clara 95054

Computer Store
820 Broadway
Santa Monica 90401

People's Computer Shop
13452 Ventura Boulevard
Sherman Oaks 91423

Computer Power and Light Company
12321 Ventura Boulevard
Studio City 91604

*Eltron
P.O. Box 2542
Sunnyvale 94087

Recreational Computer Center
1324 South Mary Avenue
Sunnyvale 94087

Tech-Mart
19590 Ventura Boulevard
Tarzana 91536

Byte Shop
2705 Thousand Oaks Boulevard
Thousand Oaks 91360

Computerland
171 East Thousand Oaks Boulevard
Thousand Oaks 91360

*California Industrial
P.O. Box 3097B
Torrance 90503

Sunny Trading Company
2530 West Sepulveda Boulevard
Torrance 90505

Computerland
104 West First Street
Tustin 92680

Computer Components Inc.
5848 Sepulveda Boulevard
Van Nuys 91411

Byte Shop
2989 North Main Street
Walnut Creek 94596

Byte Shop
8711 La Tiera Avenue
Westchester 90045

Byte Shop
14300 Beach Boulevard
Westminster 92683

• **Colorado**

Byte Shop
2040 30th Street
Boulder 80301

Intermountain Digital
1027 Dellwood Avenue
Boulder 80302

Saunders Company
3050 Valmont Road
Boulder 80301

Gateway Electronics Inc.
2839 West 44th Avenue
Denver 80211

Byte Shop
3464 South Acoma Street
Englewood 80110

• **Connecticut**

Heuristic Systems
244 Crystal Lake Road
Ellington 06029

JRV Computer Store
3714 Whitney Avenue
Hamden 06518

Computer Store
63 South Main Street
Windsor Locks 06096

• **Delaware**

Computerland
Astro Shopping Center
Kirkwood Highway
Newark 19711

Drake & Associates
1203 Flint Hill Road
Wilmington 19808

• **Florida**

*Optoelectronics, Inc.
823 South 21st Avenue
P.O. Box 219
Hollywood 33022

Byte Shop
1044 East Oakland Park Boulevard
Fort Lauderdale 33334

Douglas Computer Systems
710 Oaks Plantation Drive
Jacksonville 32211

Delta Electronics
2000 Highway 441 E
Leesburg 32748

Byte Shop
7825 Bird Road
Miami 33155

Computer Associates Inc.
6900 North Kendall Drive
Miami 33156

Economy Computing Systems
2200 Forsyth Road
Orlando 32807

Computer Stores, Inc.
2804 North Ninth Avenue
Pensacola 32502

Computer Mart
4981 72nd Avenue North
Pinellas Park 33565

Computer Age
999 S.W. 40th Avenue
Plantation 33317

Marsh Data Systems
5405 B. Southern Comfort Boulevard
Tampa 33614

Microcomputer Systems Inc.
144 South Dale Mabry Highway
Tampa 33609

Sunny Computer Stores, Inc.
117 Newton Road
West Hollywood 33123

● **Georgia**

Altair Software Distribution Center
3330 Peachtree, N.E.
Atlanta 30305

Computer Mart
5091-B Buford Highway
Atlanta 30340

The Computer Systemcenter
3330 Piedmont Road, N.E.
Atlanta 30305

● **Illinois**

Computerland
50 East Rand Road
Arlington Heights 60004

Champaign Computer Company
318 North Neil Street
Champaign 61820

The Numbers Racket
623½ South Wright Street
Champaign 61820

Aspen Computers, Inc.
7521 West Irving Park Road
Chicago 60634

Itty Bitty Machine Company
1316 Chicago Avenue
Evanston 60201

Itty Bitty Machine Company
42 West Roosevelt Road
Lombard 60148

Computerland
9511 North Milwaukee Avenue
Niles 60648

Computerland
10935 South Cicero Avenue
Oak Lawn 60453

Chicago Computer Store
517 Talcott Road
Park Ridge 60068

American Microprocessors
241 Indian Creek Road
Prairie View 60069

Data Domain
1612 East Algonquin Road
Schaumburg 60195

● **Indiana**

Data Domain
111 South College Avenue
Bloomington 47401

Hobbytronic Distributors
1218 Prairie Drive
Bloomington 47401

Data Domain
2805 East State Boulevard
Fort Wayne 46805

Quantum Computer Works
6637 Kennedy Avenue
Hammond 46323

Byte Shop
5947 East 82nd Street
Indianapolis 46250

Computers Unlimited
7724 East 89th Street
Indianapolis 46256

Data Domain
7027 North Michigan Road
Indianapolis 46268

Home Computer Center
2115 East 62nd Street
Indianapolis 46220
Audio Specialists

415 North Michigan .
South Bend 46601

Data Domain
219 West Columbia
West Lafayette 47906

● **Iowa**

The Computer Store
616 West 35th Street
Davenport 52806

● **Kansas**

Midwest Scientific Instruments Inc.
220 West Cedar
Olathe 66061

Computer Hut
21 North Hillside
Wichita 67214

Computerland
1262 North Hillside
Wichita 67214

● **Kentucky**

Data Domain
506½ Euclid Avenue
Lexington 40502

Computerland
813-B Lyndon Lane
Louisville 40222

Cybertronics
312 Production Court
Louisville 40299

Data Domain
3028 Hunsinger Lane
Louisville 40220

Logic Systems
324 West Woodlawn Avenue
Louisville 40214

● **Louisiana**

Executone Microcomputer
6969 Titian Avenue
Baton Rouge 70806

● **Maryland**

Computerland
16065 Frederick Road
Rockville 20855

Computer Workshop
5709 Frederick Avenue
Rockville 20852

Computer Workshop
11308 Hounds Way
Rockville 20852

● **Massachusetts**

*Delta Electronics
P.O. Box 2
Amesbury 01913

122

*American Used Computer Corporation
712 Beacon Street
Boston 02215

Computer Store
120 Cambridge Street
Burlington 01803

The CPU Shop
39 Pleasant Street
Charlestown 02109

*Meshna
P.O. Box 62
East Lynn 01904

*Components Group, Digital Equipment
  Corp.
One Iron Way
Marlborough 01752
(NOTE: Manufacturer sells own equipment by
  mail.)

Central Concepts
P.O. Box 272
Needham Heights 02194

*Solid State Sales
P.O. Box 74B
Somerville 02143

● **Michigan**

Compumart, Inc.
254 South Wagner Road
Ann Arbor 48103

Computer Store
310 East Washington Street
Ann Arbor 48104

*Newman Computer Exchange
1250 North Main Street
Ann Arbor 48104

Heath Company
Benton Harbor 49022
(NOTE: Company headquarters; write for
  catalog. Heathkits™ sold nationally in retail
  stores.)

Small Scale Systems
13003 Ostrander Road
Maybee 48159

*Semcom Inc.
325 South Winding Drive
Pontiac 48054

Computer Mart, Inc.
1800 West Fourteen Mile Road
Royal Oak 48073

General Computer Store
2011 Livernois
Troy 48084

● **Minnesota**

Byte Minnesota Inc.
1434 Yankee Doodle Road
Eagan 55121

Computer Room
3938 Beau D'Rue Drive
Eagan 55122

Minnesota Computers Inc.
7710 Computer Avenue, Suite 132
Edina 55435

Computer Depot, Inc.
3515 West 70th Street
Minneapolis 55435

*Digi-Key Corporation
P.O. Box 677
Thief River Falls 56701

● **Missouri**

Computer Workshop
6903 Blair Road
Kansas City 64152

K & K Company
15 East 31st Street
Kansas City 64108

Gateway Electronics
8123–25 Page Boulevard
St. Louis 63130

● **Montana**

Montana Computer Company
2512 Grande Avenue
Billings 59102

● **Nebraska**

Altair Computer Center
2801 Cornhusker Highway
Lincoln 68504

Omaha Computer Store
4540 South 84th Street
Omaha 68127

Welling Electronics
529 North 33rd Street
Omaha 68131

● **New Hampshire**

*Worldwide Electronics Inc.
10 Flagstone Drive
Hudson 03051

Computerland
419 Amherst
Nashua 03060

Computer Mart
Daniel Webster Highway, North
Merrimack 03054

● **New Jersey**

Hoboken Computer Works
20 Hudson Place
Hoboken 07030

Computer Mart
501 Highway 27
Iselin 08830

Computerland
2 De Hart Street
Morristown 07960

*Electronic Control Technology
P.O. Box 6
Union 07083

● **New York**

Computerland
1612 Niagara Falls Boulevard
Buffalo 14150

*Computer Enterprises
P.O. Box 71
Fayetteville 13066

Synchro Sound Enterprises
193–25 Jamaica Avenue
Hollis 11423

Computerland
225 Elmira Road
Ithaca 14850

Byte Shop
2721 Hempstead Turnpike
Levittown 11756

The Computer Shoppe
444 Middle Country Road
Middle Island 11953

Computer Mart
118 Madison Avenue
New York 10001

MJB Research & Development
36 West 62nd Street
New York 10023

Waco Trading Company
239 Park Avenue South
New York 10003

Comput-O-Mat Systems
41 Colby Avenue
Rye 10580

Computer Corner
200 Hamilton Avenue
White Plains 10601

● **North Carolina**

Computer Room
1729 Garden Terrace
Charlotte 28203

● **Ohio**

Ridgeway East Retail Computer Center
161 Bell Street
Chagrin Falls 44022

Data Domain
7694 Camargo Road
Cincinnati 45243

ELS Systems
2209 North Taylor Road
Cleveland Heights 44112

Computer Mart
2665 South Dixie Avenue
Dayton 45409

Data Domain
1932 Brown Street
Dayton 45409

Computerland
1304 SOM Center Road
Mayfield Heights 45412

Byte Shop
19524 Center Ridge Road
Rocky River 44116

● **Oklahoma**

High Technology
1020 West Wilshire Boulevard
Oklahoma City 74116

*Paia Electronics, Inc.
1020 West Wilshire Boulevard
Oklahoma City 74116

Global Engineering Company
5416 South Yale
Tulsa 74145

● **Oregon**

Altair Computer Center
8105 S.W. Nimbus Avenue
Beaverton 97005

Byte Shop
3482 S.W. Cedar Hills Boulevard
Beaverton 97005

Real Oregon Computer Company
205 West 10th Avenue
Eugene 97401

Byte Shop
2033 S.W. Fourth Avenue
Portland 97201

● **Pennsylvania**

Byte Shop
1045 Lancaster Pike
Bryn Mawr 19010

Artco Electronics
302 Wyoming Avenue
Kingston 18704

Personal Computer Corporation
Frazer Mall
Malvern 19355

Caldwell Computer Company
546 West Olney Avenue
Philadelphia 19120

Computer Room
Juniper & Sansome Streets
Philadelphia 19103

Computer Room
c/o Carol Groves Castle Systems
1028 Spruce Street
Philadelphia 19107

J. B. Industries
610 West Olney Avenue
Philadelphia 19120

● **Rhode Island**

Computer Power, Inc.
M 24 Airport Mall
1800 Post Road
Warwick 02886

● **South Carolina**

Computer Company
73 State Street
Charleston 29401

● **Tennessee**

Byte 'Tronics
5604 Kingston Pike
Knoxville 37919

Byte 'Tronics
1600 Hayes Street
Nashville 37203

● **Texas**

Computer World
926 North Collins
Arlington 76011

Computerland
3300 Anderson Lane
Austin 78757

Computer Shops, Inc.
211 Keystone Park
13933 North Central Expressway
Dallas 75243

Digitex
2111 Farrington Street
Dallas 75207

K. A. Electronics
1220 Majesty Drive
Dallas 75247

*Rondure Company
2522 Butler
Dallas 75237

*SD Sales Company
P.O. Box 28810
Dallas 75228

*DRC Electronics
P.O. Box 401247
Garland 75040

Altair Computer Center
12902 Harwin
Houston 77072

Byte Shop
3211 Fondren
Houston 77063

Computerland
7439 Westheimer Road
Houston 77057

Computertex
2300 Richmond Avenue
Houston 77006

Interactive Computers
7646½ Dashwood Road
Houston 77036

The MOS
1853 Richmond Avenue
Houston 77098

Neighborhood Computer Store
※20 Terrace Shopping Center
4902 34th Street
Lubbock 79410

Bit Barn
1111 Burke No. 313
Pasadena 77506

Young Electronics Service
1610 Kenwick Place
Pasadena 77505

Micro Store
634 South Central Expressway
Richardson 75080

● **Utah**

*Digital Micro Systems
P.O. Box 1212
Orem 84057

Computers & Stuff
1092 South State Street
Orem 84057

Computer Room
1455 South 1100 East
Salt Lake City 84105

Microdata Systems
796 East Lazon Drive
Sandy 84070

● **Virginia**

Computer Systems Store
1984 Chain Bridge Road
McLean 22101

Media Reactions Inc.
11303 South Shore Drive
Reston 22090

Altair Computer Center
6223 West Broad Street Road
Richmond 23230

Computer Hobbies Unlimited
9601 Kendrick Road
Richmond 23235

Home Computer Center
2927 Virginia Beach Boulevard
Virginia Beach 23452

● **Washington**

Byte Shop
14701 N.E. 20th Avenue
Bellevue 98007

Microcomputer Applications
6009-B 13th Way, S.E.
Olympia 98503

KBC Computer Shop
P.O. Box 169
Redmond 98052

Almac-Stroum
5811 Sixth Avenue South
Seattle 98108

Retail Computer Store
410 N.E. 72nd
Seattle 98115

● **West Virginia**

Computer Store
1114 Charleston National Plaza
Charleston 25301

● **Wisconsin**

Madison Computer Store
1910 Monroe Street
Madison 53711

Milwaukee Computer Store
6916 West North Avenue
Milwaukee 53213

● **Canada**

Trintronics
160 Elgin Street
Place Bell Canada
Ottawa, Ontario K2P 2C4

Computer Place
186 Queen Street West
Toronto, Ontario M5V 1Z1

First Canadian Computer Store Ltd.
44 Eglinton Avenue West
Toronto, Ontario M4R 1A1

Pacific Computer Store
4509-11 Rupert Street
Vancouver, British Columbia V5R 2J4